COUNTRY KITCHENS

THE Country Living BOOK OF
COUNTRY KITCHENS
BO NILES

Design by Jerry Demoney

A Roundtable Press Book
HEARST BOOKS • **New York**

A Roundtable Press Book

Editorial: Marsha Melnick
Directory: DuPré Cochran
Design: Jerry Demoney
Illustrations: Norman Nuding
Photo pages 8-9:
This sparsely furnished kitchen is part of a
completely restored, hundred-year-old cottage in
Kemmerer, Wyoming. Designated as a National
Historic Landmark in 1978, the turn-of-the-century
homestead is now open to the public.

Library of Congress Catalog Card Number:
85-60098
ISBN: 0-688-04267-8

Printed in Hong Kong
First Edition
1 2 3 4 5 6 7 8 9 10

Country Living's Book of Country Kitchens grew out of a desire to share the wealth of material—and especially the photography—gathered over the years at this magazine. Thanks, therefore, go to the entire staff of Country Living; everyone participates equally in the production of features for the magazine, and the work of each staffer simply made my task easier. In addition, special mention: Louise Fiore unearthed the photographs of kitchens and collections; Katie Kelly researched and wrote the pages documenting the history of the kitchen in America; Alissa Ehrenkranz researched information on the various forms of pottery so sought after by collectors today.

Susan Meyer and Marsha Melnick of Roundtable Press coordinated the editorial, design, and production of the book, and goaded me on as time flew by. Thanks, too, to Jerry Demoney for his clear and inventive design for the pages of the book, and to DuPré Cochran, for compiling and editing the exhaustive product and resource directory. Joan Nagy, Editorial Director of Hearst Books, carried the book to its publication.

Thanks, finally to Rachel Newman, editor of Country Living. Each month she shapes the magazine, granting it her special vision of what makes the spirit of country—that uniquely American spirit—endure.

Contents

What Is Country?

Country is not just a look. It is a way of life. An attitude. One phrase used frequently to describe the country look is "down-home," connoting a home environment that is authentic and natural, homespun and honest. But the country look is much more than that. The country look is America. It is our national heritage, and it has been formulated, without pretense, as this nation has grown.

The country look, in fact, has been here as long as we have. Though rooted in our colonial past, the country look is not limited merely to a legacy from the Pilgrims or the Northeast. Country comes to us through all of our ancestors, wherever they came from; it is inspired by ideas and antiques and collections from many places—not only England, but also Scandinavia, Spain and Mexico, the Middle European countries, the Orient, Africa. Elements from every culture and every country enrich the American country look and give it personality.

The history of country reaches across America, and the country look, therefore, can be created wherever you live—be it in a log cabin in Kentucky or Tennessee, an old schoolhouse in Indiana or Ohio, a solar cottage in Maine or Arizona, an adobe dwelling in New Mexico, a tract house in Oklahoma or Oregon, a beach house in the Carolinas, or a loft in New York City.

A pioneer spirit—generous, nurturing, and loving—infuses the country look. Part of that spirit derives from an intense and sincere appreciation for antiques, for ethnic country pieces collected from abroad as well as Americana. Antiques and collectibles are cherished not only for their own sake and for any intrinsic value they may have, but also as members of the family. Each piece, whether inherited or bought, is loved for its history, for the tale it tells which links its owners to the generations that have come before and those that will live on in the future. The patina of age speaks eloquently of use;

country antiques are sought after because they endure, not just because they are fashionable.

Part of the country spirit, too, grows from a love of handicraft—craft born of humble origins in many instances, craft born of necessity and ingenuity—but craft that, in its honesty, boasts a particular sophistication that is unaffected and charming. The American quilt, for example, exemplifies a painstaking attention to stitchery that is rarely reproduced with such finesse today. And the quilt also tells stories—stories of friendship, endurance, and fortitude, all stitched into the very "fabric" of the American frontier.

The country look is casual and easygoing. Of all the rooms in the house, none is more lived-in, and therefore more informal, than the kitchen. The kitchen draws everyone together, family and friends alike, through the shared rituals of preparing foods and eating. The kitchen becomes the hub for many other activities too, from homework to handicrafts. It has been called the heart of the home, and so it is.

The country kitchen is warm and cozy and welcoming, often studded with favorite antiques and collections, especially dinnerware and utensils. Beamed ceilings are favored, for they provide a place to display hanging things such as baskets and herbs. Furnishings punctuate the efficiency of the kitchen, but they are focal points as well, for additional collections or favorite small antiques such as weathervanes on pedestals, crocks, and jugs.

The table becomes almost a painting or collage in the country kitchen, allowing self-expression in many forms. Combining dinnerware with collectibles in unexpected ways is a joy to share when dining with those you care about.

In a way, the country kitchen embodies all the best of the American dream, for it is a gathering place for people of all generations; it is a haven for memories; it is a place of comfort. The sensations fostered in this place are immediate and enduring: the sight of beloved antiques; the smell and taste of foods made from recipes clipped and saved to be used again and again; the sounds of conversation and laughter; and the warm touch that inspires all the other senses in these surroundings.

The country kitchen is fantasy come true. It brings the nostalgia of heritage into the day-to-day, combining the best of both worlds.

uring the earliest days of the American colonies, the kitchen was the first room, and often the only room, to be built. Centered on the fireplace, the kitchen was at once the cooking room, the laundry room, the workroom, the schoolroom, the dining room, the bedroom—and, during bad weather, the barn for the domestic animals. As the colonies began to prosper, the American home grew. No longer a single-room dwelling, a house had other, new rooms which took on some of the specific roles first accorded to that multipurpose kitchen. The kitchen, though, still remained the warm, comforting center, and the woman of the house still spent much of her day by its cozy hearth—making food or clothing or household items, watching her children, and entertaining her friends. Even when the fireplace was replaced by a range or stove, the kitchen continued as the hub of the home.

The Early American Kitchen

The early Virginia and Massachusetts colonists began their homes with the kitchen, or "fireroom." In his history of the first new Plymouth settlement, published in 1650, Edward Johnson wrote: "[The settlers burrowed] themselves in the Earth under some Hill-side, casting the Earth aloft upon Timber; they [made] a smoaky fire against the Earth at the highest side." These homes were "miserable aboads," dark, dirt-floored, and smoky. In new settlements, where nonflammable materials were not available, the settler built a chimney out of clay and straw, and put the oven outside as a safety precaution. Later settlers made the chimney out of stone or brick and built a beehive-shaped oven into the back of the fireplace. A typical 1620s fireplace measured almost ten feet wide and four feet deep, and a built-in bench hosted many a body on chilly days.

The woodwork was probably the most attractive feature of these early homes. The kitchen floor was made out of unpainted wood (or brick, especially in the South) and left bare; rugs proved impractical because they were easily destroyed by passing feet or stray sparks. Walls were sheathed in unpainted wood; sometimes the sheathing was feather-edged or beaded. The ceiling beams were left exposed, revealing the floor of the sleeping loft overhead.

The fireroom was lit by firelight and a few tallow candles, rushlights, or grease lamps, which made the room very smoky. The first homes had no windows for light or ventilation; later houses had small, unadorned latticed windows, with oiled-paper or -linen panes. Some settlers used heavy, greenish, diamond-shaped glass panes imported from England.

Cooking around the earliest hearths was awkward and dangerous. A cook's apron or dress or arm could be burned from working in such proximity to the flames. Before cast iron was available, the colonists improvised with hardwood cooking implements, which would char and burn with repeated use. Pots and kettles hung from a heavy beam built across the flue; this so-called lug pole often burned and broke, causing the entire meal to spill into the fire. As more iron utensils were made, cooking became much easier.

Because the colonists couldn't bring many belongings to the New World, they made their own simple furnishings and equipped their houses sparsely with the bare necessities. In the kitchen stood a bench or four-legged stool, a settle by the fire, a foldaway work table of trestle or sawbuck construction, and sometimes a simple frame bed in one corner, perhaps with a trundle underneath. The work table was usually too narrow for comfortable eating, and so the family would gather around a hutch table, which doubled as a chair at other times when its top was flipped back out of the way. Food was prepared and served on a small table with drawers, or on a tavern table. The family's belongings were collected in wall shelves nailed or mortised into posts opposite the fireplace. If the fireplace was built into a gabled end, shelves could be added to each side of the fireplace.

As seventeenth-century houses grew, the fireroom was more commonly called the "kitchen." A large home had two kitchens: the original fireroom, renamed the "little kitchen" or "summer kitchen"; and a larger "great kitchen." Instead of adding to the fireroom, the southern colonists built a new house, and the old fireroom became a kitchen or bakehouse.

By the eighteenth century, the kitchen included a large cooking and work area, and also a smaller storeroom or pantry, furnished with built-in shelves and a stand, bench, or table. Much of the kitchen's woodwork remained the same, with the addition of baseboards. The oven moved to the side of the fireplace, and as a result, the size of the fireplace shrank to about six feet wide and four feet deep. A storage pit under the oven held excess ashes. The chimney wall slanted forward to generate more heat into the room. Leaning against the chimney wall, a large iron fireback with a fancy raised design reflected heat and protected the masonry from the intense temperatures of the fire.

The 1700s kitchen was light and comfortable. With smoke-darkened ceilings and walls now whitewashed clean, and the window openings cut to fit eight-over-twelve or twelve-over-twelve pane sashes, this room welcomed fresh air and sunshine.

A gamut of iron, copper, brass, and tin cooking utensils simplified hearth cooking. The swinging crane, which held pots and kettles over the fire, could be adjusted to lift the pots away from the flame or to tend the food.

American furnishings blossomed in the eighteenth and early nineteenth centuries. Much of the country furniture so prized by collectors today was made during this period. The country furniture makers simplified and adapted European styles to fit the more modest American dwelling. Windsor furniture was especially popular in the colonies. Its simple forms perfectly suited the early eighteenth-century homes, and the Windsor chair was comfortable for working in the kitchen, as its gently curved seat and splay back offered more support than a bench or stool.

Other kitchen furnishings included specially crafted pieces used for storage. Cupboards fit neatly into corners or against the wall, while smaller varieties were hung directly on the wall. Some cupboards had doors, while others openly displayed the family's tableware. Flour and dough bins stored makings for the daily bread, and just-baked pies and breads stayed fresh in pie safes with punched-tin panels. Dry sinks were filled with water to wash dishes, laundry, and vegetables.

This Wisconsin kitchen was built by a Danish settler in 1872. Furnishings are typically spare and utilitarian. The table near the window probably served as a work counter. Antique kitchenware sits on open shelves.

The technology resulting from innovations spawned by the Industrial Revolution completely changed the look of the country kitchen. In the late 1700s, Sir Benjamin Thompson, known as Count Rumford, designed the first range, a brick U-shaped cooking apparatus on which pots and pans were placed over a concentrated heat source. As soon as it was possible for furnaces to cast stoves out of pig iron, cookstoves and ranges were made in quantity to be shipped and sold all across the country. By 1881, more than a thousand stove patents had been issued, and there were 220 stove manufacturers in business. These cookstoves burned coal, wood, and even corncobs; later they used kerosene or natural gas. The temperature of the cookstove wasn't easy to control; many a cook tested the oven by inserting her forearm in its mouth for almost one minute! Although many homemakers welcomed the cookstove, others missed the great hearth. In 1869 author/home economist Harriet Beecher Stowe asked, "Would our Revolutionary fathers have gone barefooted and bleeding over snows to defend airtight stoves and cooking ranges? I trow not. It was the memory of the great open kitchen fire . . . that called to them through the snows of that dreadful winter."

The "great open fire" was not the only kitchen feature to be replaced by modern ingenuity. To preserve fresh foods longer, the first primitive refrigerator was built in 1834. It was merely a zinc- or tin-lined wooden box with the space between the lining and the box filled with powdered charcoal. Special storage spaces held up to a hundred pounds of ice. The water from the melted ice escaped through a drain hole in the base of the icebox. Later iceboxes, upright and chest versions, sported built-in water coolers, matching sideboards and china closets, walls insulated with ground cork, or slate shelves.

Plumbing modernized the dry sink. The new kitchen sink was made of water-resistant iron, soapstone, wood, granite, or crockery. The June 1899 issue of the *Ladies Home Journal* said, "A galvanized iron sink is quite the best cheap sink obtainable, provided it has a galvanized back . . . ."

Many cooks began suggesting ways to improve the design of the kitchen. Catharine E. Beecher and Harriet Beecher Stowe wrote one of the first books on home economics—*The American Woman's Home; or, Principles of Domestic Science as Applied to the Duties and Pleasures of Home,* published in 1869. They said, "The kitchen should be like the cook's galley in a steamship, every article and utensil used in cooking . . . so arranged that with one or two steps the cook can reach all he needs." With this in mind, the Stowe sisters designed a detailed layout of kitchen equipment and furniture, featuring innovative built-in cabinets and a sink with adjacent cutting board and dish drainer.

The mid- to late-1800s kitchen was a bright, warm, cozy place. Potted plants and chintz or white muslin curtains decorated the windows. The walls were painted or whitewashed, and the woodwork painted or grained. The floors were left plain or sometimes covered in easy-to-clean linoleum; lignum, a cork fiber; or lignotec, a wood fiber. Cheap rag rugs, which were made at home or bought from country peddlers, colored the floor. The kitchen table, left plain or painted, was covered with linoleum to match the

floor, or with an oilcloth. Factory-made chairs, particularly bentwood, joined the older country varieties. Through all seasons, the cookstove burned next to a well-stocked wood or coal box.

At the turn of the century, the Midwestern-produced "Hoosier," or "Dutch," cabinet added storage space to the kitchen. Many designs included a built-in flour bin with sifter, a spice rack, a cookbook rack, and even a porcelain-enameled work surface. Hoosier cabinets were touted by their makers to be "as necessary in the kitchen as a stove," and practically every American home had one. By the early 1900s, the Hoosier was replaced by built-in cabinets.

The summer kitchen of Massachusett's Merrell Tavern, built in the 1790s, retains some of its original furnishings. These include the marble hearth slabs, the swinging crane, and the Federal-style table.

The Kitchen Today

The twentieth century brought dramatic technological changes to the kitchen. Built-in cabinetry and smooth, easy-to-clean surfaces streamlined the look of the kitchen. Modern appliances, from the dishwasher to the electric toaster, shortened and eased the time spent in the kitchen. Although these changes were welcomed, the kitchen lost some of its warmth and country charm. Today, many kitchens, using antique or reproduction furnishings, look back to the seventeenth, eighteenth, and nineteenth centuries for comfort and inspiration. These old-fashioned, country-spirited kitchens are featured in the following chapters.

A settler's kitchen in Tennessee might have looked like this one, which dates from 1790, and is now part of the Museum of Appalachia in Norris, Tennessee. The mantel, typical of Appalachian fireplaces, is dressed with a skirt down both sides. The gourds on top were used as dippers or to hold sugar, salt, or eggs.

The creativity and imagination with which people design and decorate their kitchens—or remodel them—is boundless. No two kitchens, even when they both have country style, ever really look alike because the individual personalities of their owners shine through. Within the general work plan, antique furnishings supplement storage and surfaces, with cupboards holding utensils and collections, and tables adding their own dimension for displaying beloved objects or acting as extra work counters. The best kitchens work on every level: They function efficiently; they lend an air of intimacy and invitation; they show off favorite possessions—and they do it all harmoniously. Country kitchens may reflect regional tastes, and they may appear either streamlined or brim-full, but they always radiate a sense of comfort that is down-to-earth.

Great Country Kitchens

The more rustic aspects of the country look are derived from an attraction to raw materials from the land—especially wood and stone—which become the background for many kitchens throughout the United States. The log cabin and the stone cottage, even today, are being reproduced for the same reason as in days of old. Logs and stone are sturdy and solid, warm and enduring, in tune with a pioneering spirit and a down-home mood.

Log cabins need not be old to convey a sense of authenticity and age. This particular log home, in a suburban area outside Atlanta, was recently constructed from a kit. The logs were notched together neatly, and logs of like dimensions were selected to form the truss support system for the ceilings and roof as well. At one end of the cabin's 37-foot-long keeping room lies the kitchen, outfitted all in wood to harmonize with the logs. The kitchen is ample in scale, not only to give enough room for cooking activities, but also to accommodate burgeoning collections. A grand center island anchors the room; it has a cooktop conveniently positioned directly opposite the double-bowl sink. Cabinets run under the counters only, and so additional storage was arranged in a series of antique pieces—a step-back cupboard, a pie safe, and a dough box. Open shelving around the window was allocated as the display area for a collection of salt-glazed pottery.

In a kitchen that embraces many collections, baskets ride in rows along the ceiling beams, leaving room for herbs to hang beneath without obstruction.

Fresh Herb Vinegars

You can use virtually any herb to make vinegar, but the following are favorites: sweet basil, purple basil, thyme, tarragon, lovage, mint, sweet marjoram, bay laurel, rosemary, chive blossoms, dill, oregano, and salad burnett (tastes like cucumbers).

1 gallon cider or white vinegar
Well-rinsed fresh herbs

1. Pour off and reserve about half the contents of the vinegar jug. Cider vinegar suits every kind of herb except purple basil and chive blossoms. These colorful herbs, when steeped in white vinegar, produce a beautiful, delicate pink vinegar.

2. Stuff the jug as full as possible with herbs. Top off the jug with some of the reserved vinegar; cover and place in the sun to steep for about three weeks, or until vinegar is nicely flavored. The jug of chive-blossom vinegar should be placed in a brown bag and steeped in a dark place.

3. Funnel off vinegar into smaller bottles, placing a fresh snippet of the herb used in each bottle. Label bottles and store in a cool, dark place.

Log-Home Manufacturers

Alta Industries
P.O. Box 88
Halcottsville, NY
12438

American Lincoln
Homes
P.O. Box 669
Battleboro, NC
27809

Authentic Homes
Corp.
Box 1288
Laramie, WY 82070

Boyne Falls Log
Homes Inc.
Boyne Falls, MI
49713

Hearthstone Log
Homes
Route 2, Box 434
Dandridge, TN
37725

Lincoln Logs Ltd.
Gristmill Road
Chestertown, NY
12817

Lok-n-Logs
RD#2
Sherburne, NY
13460

New England Log
Homes
2301 State Street
P.O. Box 5056
Hamden, CT 06518

Northern Products
Log Homes

P.O. Box 616
Bomarc Road
Bangor, ME 04401

Rocky Mountain Log
Homes
3353 Highway 93
South
Hamilton, MT 59840

Timber Log Homes
P.O. Box 300
Austin Drive
Marlborough, CT
06447

Town & Country Log
Homes
U.S. 131 South
Petoskey, MI 49770

Ward Cabin
Company
P.O. Box 72
Houlton, ME 04730

Wilderness Log
Homes
Route 2
Plymouth, WI 53073

Wisconsin Log
Homes
P.O. Box 11005
Green Bay, WI 54307

For further information

Log Home Guide
Information Center
U.S. 40
Hartford, TN 37753

To amplify the dimensions of an eighteenth-century stone mill house in Pennsylvania, a log cabin dating from 1730 was removed, log by log, from its original site in a nearby county and reassembled as an annex to the house. Time-honored construction techniques were respected, including the application of a particular masonry mix for chinking that was based on horsehair and pebbles. The log annex is devoted to the kitchen and an adjoining mudroom. Logs graphically define the newly restored space, with bright bands of white chinking between. Wide floorboards were given a lustrous sheen with layers of polyurethane. New planking linking the ceiling beams was paled to visually lift the ceiling and add light to the room. A wood stove, made in Gettysburg in 1800, warms the kitchen and complements the cooktop and oven across the room; foods can be maintained at an even temperature if placed on top of the stove behind the pipe. Major appliances were enameled with red, as was the reproduction tin chandelier. The red dignifies the room and actually lessens the impact of the size of the appliances, because it marries with the deeper reds in the panels on adjacent cabinet doors.

A blue ladder-back chair cues in the color scheme in this log kitchen. The blue, which washes both the under-counter cabinets and the framing around the window, is offset by the red in the appliances, and also by a subtler red used on panels on the cabinet doors. The double-heart motif is common to this part of Pennsylvania.

Log and Stone Kitchens

A log cabin dating from the 1790s was hauled to an old family homestead in northwestern South Carolina, and then spliced to a one-room schoolhouse to form a cozy year-round home. The schoolhouse converted neatly into a kitchen (with adjoining pantry, bath, and screened-in porch). Interior walls were constructed of the same wide planking as the ceiling and floors; all the wood was turned inside out to reveal its smooth, untouched face. The uniform tonality is a gentle foil for the energetic ikat-style fabric used on the loveseat. The loveseat faces a fieldstone fireplace and coaxes family and friends into the kitchen at any excuse. Barn siding sheathes the cabinets and also the dishwasher and oven. The nonworking cast-iron wood stove, a relic cherished for its robust personality, stands next to the pantry and is used to display a collection of antique utensils, and a graniteware coffeepot.

Southern-style biscuits, some gathered under a protective wire dome to insure against an invasion of hungry flies, and turnovers and bread were baked in old tinware to be served from a baker's table during a brunch. The red chinking between logs is indigenous to this part of South Carolina.

Local antiques and family heirlooms fill this log house and establish a focal point for the kitchen, especially the two-board heart-pine kitchen table with its original blue paint. The coffee bin just behind the table came out of a nearby store.

Log and Stone Kitchens

Newly built by an artist for his family, this log cabin set in the woods in Washington State subscribes absolutely to the view that honesty in decor is the best policy. In other words, everything in the house is accessible to everyone all the time. This notion applies especially to the kitchen, which was designed with walls of open shelving so that foods and dishes would be always within reach, and also to display all the homemade preserves that the family is proud to share. The shelves stand out in bold relief against the log walls, and the stacked supplies look almost like colorful sculptures. Wire bins slide in where necessary to hold small and shallow items. An architect's lamp clips onto the shelf over the range, its elbow swinging with enough flexibility to light up counters on either side too. Cabinets under the counters store garbage pails and other less frequently used or less attractive necessities. The countertops, contrasting with the all-wood theme, were tiled in blue ceramic squares grouted in gray. The window over the sink pivots outward so that it can be utilized as a pass-through to the deck and yard.

Textures and colors capture the eye in this wide-open kitchen and set off the gentle ripples of the log walls. Logs here are wedded by strips of wood rather than by chinking, and so the tonality of the wood remains pure and consistent.

Potato Bread

2 tablespoons sugar	1 1/2 cups mashed
4 teaspoons salt	potatoes
2 packages active	milk
dry yeast	1/4 cup butter or
about 8 cups all-	margarine
purpose flour	2 eggs
1/2 cup water	

About 4 hours before serving or up to 3 days ahead.

1. In large bowl, combine sugar, salt, yeast, and 1 1/2 cups flour. In 2-quart saucepan mix water, mashed potatoes, and 1 1/2 cups milk; add butter or margarine; over low heat, heat until very warm (120° to 130°F), stirring often. (Butter or margarine does not need to melt completely.) With mixer at low speed, gradually beat liquid into dry ingredients just until blended; beat in eggs. Increase speed to medium; beat 2 minutes, occasionally scraping bowl. Beat in 1 cup flour to make a thick batter; continue beating 2 minutes, scraping bowl often. Stir in enough additional flour (about 3 1/4 cups) to make a soft dough.

2. Turn dough onto well-floured surface and knead about 10 minutes until smooth and elastic, kneading in about 1 1/2 cups flour. Shape into ball; place in greased large bowl, turning over so that top is greased. Cover; let rise in warm place (80° to 85°F), away from draft, until doubled, about 1 hour. (Dough is doubled when fingers pressed into it leave a dent.)

3. Punch down dough; turn onto lightly floured surface; cut dough in half; cover with towel for 15 minutes and let rest.

4. Grease two 2-quart round, shallow casseroles. Shape one piece of dough into ball; place in casserole. Cut two parallel slashes on top. Repeat. Cover; let rise in warm place until doubled, about 1 hour.

5. Preheat oven to 400°F. Brush each loaf with milk. Bake 40 minutes, or until well-browned and loaves sound hollow when tapped. Remove from casseroles immediately; cool on racks. Makes two 2 1/4 pound loaves.

Log and Stone Kitchens

A nineteenth-century homestead deep in the heart of Texas hill country included a derelict barn. The proportions of the barn were good, and its limestone walls were unusual in their texture, and so it was decided to transform the barn into a full-scale house. The downstairs comprises an open-plan living/dining/cooking area. At the center of one wall in the big room is the original opening where livestock used to enter; this aperture is now closed off by a pair of screened doors, but the old barn doors still slide into place on the outside of the barn, in lieu of conventional wooden doors. The limestone inside was scrubbed down to remove any reminder of the former four-footed inhabitants, and in the kitchen only a few wall-hung cabinets were installed so that the stone could be seen and enjoyed fully. Beams in the kitchen, hand-hewn and hand-pegged, were hollowed out so that water pipes and electrical wiring could run along inside to the appropriate appliances without disturbing the decor. Old floorboards were retained wherever possible, softened by rag and hooked rugs. The cylindrical butcher block proves a useful way station for foods and dishes on their way to or from the living/dining area. Counters, which have been cut extra deep, garage trays, utensils, jars, and other goods.

The Country Charm wood stove that warms the cozy kitchen corner in this stone house is also used for cooking and baking. Periodic tune-ups and regular cleaning keep it quirk-free as well as resplendent in its utilitarian beauty.

Regional Kitchens

Because of the migrations of different peoples to different parts of the United States, the country look, with its roots in ethnic heritage, varies widely. Mexican and Spanish influences, for instance, can be felt throughout the Southwest and in California; Scandinavian touches are in evidence in towns near the ocean and near the Great Lakes of the North; and, in parts of Texas, where German immigrants came to settle, souvenirs remain of an Old World that will never be forgotten, but instead will be cherished forever.

This updated kitchen on a sheep farm in rural Pennsylvania represents the most traditional and expected of all American country looks: It is the quintessential New England-style kitchen. Ruddy wood tones prevail in the room, harmonizing with classic barn red and other harvest colors. These colors show up in the distinctive stenciled borders that run just beneath the ceiling, along the baseboard, and above the chair rail. The stenciling, based on old New England patterns, unifies the two areas of the room. Local antiques, such as the sawbuck table used for dining, were chosen for their specifically cozy appeal. Humorous asides—in the form of sheep—crop up on tableware and in folk art. At the small-paned windows: a ubiquitous checked pattern favored in many country kitchens, here rendered in mustard.

Simplicity, honesty, and warmth are prevailing themes in the kitchen. Furnishings are spare and plain, and accessories modest and pure in shape and function, especially the collection of baskets hanging from the beam over the peninsula.

A 1760 house within walking distance of the ocean in New England needed a face-lift, and this was effected through a Scandinavian approach to construction and decoration. Key to this particular style is a preference for pale woods, open shelving, and for pure paint-box colors used in ways both expected and out-of-the-ordinary. In this kitchen, the open shelving is birch, as are the cabinets; a blue wall covering lines the back wall of the shelving and sets off the variety of kitchen things stored there. The same blue pulsates across the floor and then occurs again in the selection of glassware and linens. A pastel yellow sparkles around the windows and then pops up in pieces of pottery and even in the bucket used for soaking fresh flowers before cutting and arranging them. A rag rug brings out the full range of colors viewed in the kitchen; rag rugs are as common to Scandinavia as they are to the United States, although many there are used as runners, either singly or in series.

The desire for light and color is immediately apparent, through the selection of paint colors, dinnerware, and accessories.

Regional Kitchens

The year-round sun and temperate climate of southern California suggest a lifestyle that capitalizes on a love of the outdoors. The California style is naturally vibrant and sumptuous in its sweep of space and alluring use of light, yet it is intimate in its attention to detail. Traditionally oriented toward a Mediterranean look—in combination with Mexican motifs and provincial accents—the California kitchen is often hospitably eclectic. This one certainly is. It uses Mexican quarry tile underfoot, and French provincial ceramic tiles on countertops and backsplashes. The provincial mood continues in the cabinetry, custom-styled after French country furniture. Panels cut to match the cabinets fit over appliances as well. The cabinets were planned for maximum efficiency; a corner cabinet, for example, opens to a lazy susan, and an extra board on which to set groceries pulls out next to the refrigerator. Porcelain knobs with wrought-iron wings add an Old World accent to doors and drawers. A larger-than-usual window pulls in plenty of sunlight to nourish a collection of flowering plants.

A robust worktable is a dramatic, yet warm-hearted, focal point in the kitchen and serves equally well for food preparation and, when necessary, for dining.

A love of pattern- and color-energized fabric and paper is a hallmark of the provincial style, in France and in England alike. This eighty-year-old kitchen in a suburb near the Atlantic Ocean employs pattern throughout to invigorate the space. Fabric separates the kitchen from an adjoining dining room, accenting the opening and softening the definition of the break between. Hunter green, a prominent color in the pattern, is picked up in wood trim and also in the plastic laminate covering the countertops. Wormy chestnut cabinets, with their unique pitting, harmonize in tone with the warm wood flooring and carefully chosen provincial antiques such as the harvest table and the dresser in the dining room. Brick facing climbs behind the cooktop and continues along under the window over the sink; the bricks were treated to resist grease and water marks. The island in the kitchen proper, converted from an old dry sink and capped with butcher block provides a supplementary work surface but also functions as a buffet for large gatherings. An antique meat rack hangs over the island, displaying baskets and copper pots made in France.

Patterns abound in this provincial-style kitchen. Various types of pottery, including a collection of fanciful majolica from England, play off against the mini-prints and add dashes of bright color to the decor.

Brilliant sun, dazzling sky, and soft desert hues are synonymous with the textures and tones resonant in the art and architecture of the American Southwest. A kitchen in Santa Fe calls all these influences into play. Though newly built, the house was modeled after its adobe antecedents, and, true to form, wherever an aperture appears—such as a window recess or a doorway opening—the edges are gently defined. The adobe clay has been daubed over in white to reflect the natural light pouring onto the tiled island from overhead skylights. This island, grand in scale, is faced in blue Mexican ceramic squares. These repeat along the backsplash and again on a hot-pot insert next to the sink. Blond wood accent strips set off the tiles and match the wooden countertop section. Mexican quarry tiles typically used throughout the Southwest blanket the floor.

For variety in cooking methods, the kitchen has two heavy-duty cooktops—one a professional gas unit and the other, on the island, an electric one. All shelving for kitchenwares and spices is open to view.

American Indian pots from about A.D. 1200 adorn display shelves, their graphics both bold and sensitive. The general blue-and-white theme is carried out in a selection of bowls and other serving pieces which fill an open rack salvaged from a shoe factory.

Fredericksburg, a town deep in the hill country of Texas, was founded by a group of German pioneers in the middle of the last century. The German influence—in architecture, furnishings, and accessories—prevails in many homes. This particular kitchen, though not in one of the original houses, still demonstrates a German influence in its fastidious attention to the planning of the space, as well as in some of its fine collectibles. Cabinets on one wall balance with two cupboards against the wall opposite, one a corner piece and one a step-back. The mix works with great efficiency, keeping all kitchen and dinnerware supplies within easy reach of the Mennonite table in the center of the space and close enough, too, to the dining area next door. On the dining porch, huge screened windows temper breeze and sun in this often-torrid climate; a softly gathered valance runs across the top.

One unique reminder of the old country is the German flour jar standing on the table; pieces such as this one are handed down through the generations and cherished for their memories as well as their utilitarian value.

Kitchen Additions

The primary room to be remodeled, and often the first room to be added on to an existing house, is usually the kitchen. In the most practical sense, the kitchen is the soul of the house, and creating an addition that will accommodate a kitchen also accommodates the most tangible needs of any family—food and drink.

A small shed attached to a carriage house on the Delaware Canal was converted into a compact and cozy kitchen. The appliances combine naturally along an L, with the sink turning the corner to retain sufficient storage below. The L was measured a bit short on purpose to allow shallow shelves at one end, near the door to the kitchen, where jars are displayed. The appliances relate directly to the island, which is actually a sculptor's table dating from the early 1900s. The range and refrigerator take advantage of its grandiose surface for preparation of foods and for distribution of groceries after marketing. A full supply of pots and pans hangs over the island from butchers' racks.

The dining side of the island is situated near the dishwasher so that plates can be removed easily after eating, and the view from this position, through a pair of French doors, is beautiful. Overhead skylights dispel gloom; mini-slat blinds reel down along special tracks to counteract any glare. Pumpkin pine floorboards, installed over former dirt floors, were slicked with polyurethane for protection against dirt.

Animal collections add cheer to this cottage kitchen. A sheep strides along a beam over the French doors; a cow hangs on the lid of a cardboard egg sorter on the counter; and a mini-herd grazes in a mail sorter behind the range.

Grafting a new kitchen wing onto an 1870s suburban house vastly improved the layout of the house as a whole and particularly the cooking setup. The room capitalizes on its southern exposure with pairs of extra-large windows. Broken by mullions into twelve-over-twelve sashes, the windows assume a colonial aspect. Matchstick blinds unfurl over the panes when the sun strikes hottest, especially during the summer months.

The focal point in the new room is the luxurious island, which contains both the cooktop and a double-bowl sink. Venting down and under the island eliminates the need for an intrusive overhead hood. The sink has a soap dispenser, a spray attachment, and a bar faucet instead of the standard type, so that dishes can be washed and rinsed more easily. Delft tiles surround both appliances for use as a hot-top and chopping surface.

The settee in the window was picked up at a local flea market and spruced up with a new coat of paint to match the blue in the stenciled floorcloths. Napkins drape over the edge of the island in lieu of place mats. Recessed lights, set between the ceiling beams and controlled by rheostats, spotlight the various areas.

The mellow tone of wood is echoed in the paneling inserted into the doors of the refrigerator/freezer and is also balanced by the prancing carousel horse, which was stripped of its paint to reveal the honey color beneath.

This barn in upstate New York was so large that it was possible to engineer an addition right inside the huge space by inserting a new mezzanine level along two walls. This area, reached by an open stair from the living room, houses the kitchen and two separate eating areas. The kitchen, tucked into the corner of the L-shaped balcony, is convenient to both areas because its peninsula serves one while a handmade butcher-block island serves the other. Two alcoves were designed to shelter the refrigerator and the restaurant range; the range hood hides under the eaves, sucking smoke out of the barn with barely a whisper. Next to the stove is the pantry, which keeps all foods and household goods out of sight. Barn siding, turned inside out to its smooth face, forms cabinet fronts and is used on the window wall. The countertops, also hand-sawn from barn siding, were treated with polyurethane, as were the wide-plank pine floors. The base cabinets cantilever over high, deep-set bases, both to prevent bumping toes and to elevate the cabinets so the work surface would be at a more suitable height for the tall owners. Stucco, roughly troweled onto the walls and ceiling, emphasizes the rusticity of the barn. Three new windows were inserted over the restaurant-gauge sink to take in views of the fields; a narrow shelf stretches over the three, tying them together visually and providing a showcase for a collection of plates. Drawers next to the sink become deeper and deeper, depending upon what they hold, from cutlery to flour.

The deliberate selection of all-white kitchenware and dishes gives all the woods in the barn "breathing" room, by offering no distraction in pattern or tone.

Often the country look is construed as being limited, nostalgic, and old-fashioned in aspect and appeal. Nothing could be farther from the truth; country kitchens that capitalize on contemporary design can be infused with warmth and texture—it is just that the silhouette of cabinetry, for example, may appear streamlined, or perhaps clusters of collectibles or crafts may display a particular sophistication and sensibility that is derived from clarity rather than clutter. Contemporary country kitchens are harmonious, blending efficiency and sincerity in a search for a purer statement of style.

A house in Westchester County, New York, was gutted at one end to make way for an expanded kitchen; with two rooms turned into one and the ceiling raised to the roof line, the kitchen developed into a magnificent and streamlined space. Beams were retained and stained dark, as were the planks linking them. The oak flooring, by contrast, was left pale because two dark surfaces would have "sandwiched" the room—top to bottom—and made it feel small. Cabinets were tailored and installed to be congruent with the height of an antique step-back cupboard, and their coloring clearly matches the original paint inside this particular piece of furniture. Luckily, too, the tops of the cabinets also align with that of the refrigerator/freezer and of the sliding glass door leading to the deck. The clean surface that resulted overhead is the perfect background for a collection of baskets. An island houses the cooktop; its backsplash and the under-counter venting system contained there shield the appliance from the adjoining dining area. Track lighting was painted to mirror the cabinets, and the fixtures appear almost invisible as they ride along the ceiling.

The discipline of this carefully crafted kitchen is reflected in the choice of accessories, many of which display a rigorous attention to checks and grids—in the game boards, for example, and basket weaves, and even in the pattern of the rag runner and dish towel.

Contemporary Kitchens

A newly constructed Victorian-style house outside Seattle capitalizes on the Northwestern penchant for woods, especially in the kitchen. The woods clarify the space—they don't compress it—and this happens because the tonality is honey-pale. Cabinetry reaches all the way to the ceiling for a clean silhouette; there is no hardware either, which reinforces the clutter-free look. The flooring, which matches the cabinetry in hue, is enlivened by dark pegs that emphasize the length of each plank. The main energy in the room is derived from the jazzy checkerboard pattern of the tiled backsplash and countertop. The backsplash is extra-high to accommodate small appliances underneath the pushed-up wall cabinets; because of the added room then, these appliances do not have to be tugged out from the wall in order to be used. Plants diffuse light at the window, obviating any need for blinds or shades. The double-bowl sink, just under the window, has twin dispensers—one for boiling water and one for ice water—in addition to the rotating high-spout faucet. The "butcher-block" telephone was installed to be as accessible to the family room as it is to the kitchen itself.

Wood appears both contemporary and cozy in this kitchen because it is used to dramatize the absolute simplicity of the room. The edge trim on the cabinet doors looks like old picture frames, and the floors appear as if they had been hand-pegged.

Contemporary Kitchens

Barn-wood siding, typically chosen for its weathered rusticity, appears sleek and almost futuristic in this California house because it evenly blankets walls, cabinets, and even the range hood. Laminate simulating the same textures zips across the countertops and island for further unity. Stainless-steel appliances blend harmoniously with the muted gray tone of the siding, complemented by a rose paint that arcs up from above the window and covers the ceiling. Lighting is carefully positioned to cast a glow where needed, especially over the restaurant range and sink. The island is shaped like an L, which offers two extra sides for food preparation so that two or more cooks can work together comfortably and not get in each other's way. At the indentation of the L on the island is an additional sink that is convenient to the butcher-block inset; vegetables can be washed and chopped, therefore, at the same time that dishes across the way are rinsed. The island, too, is ringed by lots of drawers, each organized and divided according to what will be stored there, from cutlery to linens to spices and exotic foods.

A kitchen that can mimic a barn with both wood and laminate, and also add a command to "get fed" in tandem with a stuffed rooster, refreshes with its innate sense of humor. The E-A-T letters came out of an English pub, and they fit perfectly between the window and the ceiling in the room.

The house may be old—over a hundred and twenty years old, in fact—but the impact of its interiors is highly modern. Slick white paint emphasizes the clear space, and a wide swath of windows further enhances the space by harnessing huge doses of daylight. The paint sheaths old cabinets, which were formerly dark brown, and makes them appear brand-new; architectural pulls reinforce the notion of newness. Track lighting is unobtrusive yet pinpoints work surfaces and the dining area with precision. Highly glazed blue tiles both surprise and soothe with their cool color; and the blue is so strong that no rug is necessary to break its flow. The kitchen's country manners are retained through the selection of fine primitive furnishings and accessories, which offer their rustic textures as an antidote to the crisp white-and-blue scheme.

This country kitchen functions efficiently, yet warmly, because the balance of new and old is exact and graceful. Things used for cooking are always new; those used for serving are old.

Old-Fashioned Buttermilk Biscuits

These feathery-light, golden biscuits are bigger than usual so that you can spread plenty of honey on them or sop up delicious gravy.

Makes about 1 dozen biscuits

3 cups unbleached all-purpose flour	*1 teaspoon salt*
1 tablespoon baking powder	*2/3 cup butter-flavor or regular vegetable shortening*
1/2 teaspoon baking soda	*1 1/4 to 1 1/3 cups buttermilk*

1. Heat oven to 450°F. In large bowl, with pastry blender or two knives used scissor-fashion, mix flour, baking powder, baking soda, and salt. Cut in shortening until mixture resembles coarse crumbs.

2. With fork, stir in buttermilk just until mixture forms a soft dough and leaves side of bowl.

3. On lightly floured surface with lightly floured hands, knead dough 10 minutes. With rolling pin, roll dough into 1/2-inch thickness. With floured 3-inch round cutter, cut as many biscuits as possible. Place them about 1/2 inch apart on large cookie sheet. Press dough trimmings together; roll and cut as above until all dough is cut. Bake biscuits 10 to 12 minutes until golden brown.

Quick Buttermilk Biscuits. In bowl, combine *3 cups buttermilk baking mix* with *1 cup milk* until soft dough forms. If dough is too sticky, gradually mix in more baking mix to make dough easy to handle. Knead, roll, cut, and bake as above.

Many city dwellers like to bring the country home—partly as an escape from the noise and bustle of the outside environment, and partly in response to the objects they care for most and want to keep around them in their most intimate surroundings. Country kitchens, therefore, are as open and fresh in apartments as they are in houses. Air and light are the main ingredients; the scent of down-home cooking is rarely far behind.

One big square room that extends across the rear half of a walk-up apartment in Manhattan combines the living and dining areas with the kitchen. The room feels spacious, partly because it is highly organized, with everything in its place, but also because it relies on a simple color scheme: bright white in tandem with a rustic turquoise blue. White washes all the surfaces, including bleached wood and tiled floors. The blue pops up in selected antiques, one of which is an extra-long dry sink that performs the multiple functions of room divider, buffet, countertop, and storage unit. The actual kitchen runs along one wall of the room, with the sink, dishwasher, range, and under-counter refrigerator and freezer in a line-up. A thick butcher-block counter tops the group. The range hood sandwiches neatly between thin tiers of open shelving, venting smoke and odors behind the wall to the outdoors. Canvas blinds, pulling up from the bottom, assure privacy while letting in as much light as possible.

The use of whiteware on the shelves reduces any sense of clutter in this one-wall kitchen, while an antique knife rack and a collection of useful sponge ware generate a feeling of caring and coziness.

Texturing a Wall

Instead of installing a wall covering to achieve a textured effect for your kitchen walls, you can paint them in a number of ways. First, set down a primary base coat of paint and allow it to dry thoroughly. For the best results when comb painting, use a gloss or semigloss paint underneath. For sponging or stippling, a flat paint is perfectly suitable.

Sponging. You can use any ordinary household sponge as long as it is very porous and you can squeeze it almost dry. Dense sponges will leave flat marks. To achieve an open, frothy look, dip one end of the sponge into your paint and then squeeze or tap it almost dry on a paper towel; you will be able to visually judge the mark you will make on the wall if you do dab it on the towel first. Apply the marks in any pattern you choose, dipping and dabbing frequently so that your sponge marks will remain consistent across the wall surface.

Stippling. A thin-tipped paintbrush, the kind usually used by artists for oil painting, works best. Dip the brush into your paint and wipe off any excess drips, and then apply dots in any pattern you wish—either evenly spaced or dabbed on at random. Stippling can be very interesting if you "build up" your dots. Go back over an area you have already worked, and add more dots. You can use the same color, applied with a lighter or darker touch, to create shadow effects, or you can add different colors for more of a glow.

Combing. Work only a small section of the wall at a time, for the second coat of paint must be very wet to comb through it. Layer the second coat of paint evenly across this section of wall. Then, pull or drag a wide, flat-tined comb (available at art and craft supply shops and at specialty paint stores) across the wet paint in linear or wavy patterns. Dry off the comb repeatedly so that it will not build up a gooey residue, which can slip back into the combed areas. You can work your way across the wall or from ceiling to floor, depending on the effect desired.

Country-in-the-City Kitchens

An amusing and casually coordinated interplay of pattern on pattern enlivens a diminutive kitchen located behind a big-city antique shop. As the kitchen is used only for lunches and coffee breaks, its needs were uncomplicated: to provide an occasional omelette or a cup of coffee or tea, or perhaps a piece of fruit for late-afternoon energy. For this reason, the old stove, which functions perfectly for simple tasks, was left right where it was, as was the sink. Changes were merely cosmetic, but fun: The walls were sponge-painted to complement the original speckled linoleum tile floor, as well as the collection of sponge and graniteware which is used daily. Humorous touches include a strawberry hot pad over the sink, old-time milk bottles still resting in their wire carryall, and a barbershop lantern which lights the whole room. Narrow but thick shelves, spliced in between the existing jogs around the walls, display all collectibles.

A painted primitive hutch table, well worn from rugged use, stands at the center of the kitchen and welcomes all comers to a cup of coffee. Colors throughout the room, based on a palette of pale greens, seem to fuse, even though nothing was painted at the same time.

61

Country-in-the-City Kitchens

Bigger than many typically found in the city, this eat-in kitchen allows ample room for cooking, even with small children in tow. But the original layout of the kitchen did not allow much storage space, and the appliances had to be planned to lock into the existing grid of gas, electrical, and plumbing lines. Paint, fabric, and flooring have been used to even out dissimilarities—in the way everything looked. A resilient floor designed to resemble tile runs underfoot and ties in unobtrusively with new barn-red doors and trim. The ruddiness continues in the choice of wood for open shelving and base cabinets to harmonize with a favorite stepback cupboard. A cheerful gingham check fabric lines all the shelving, new and old, and acts as a unifying backdrop for a disparate collection of pottery, china, and books. Although the appliances couldn't be relocated, they were moved out from the wall slightly to allow an extra shelf to run along behind. Here, the flatware, spices, and a toaster oven assemble, right within reach but out of range of stove-top spatters. A kerosene lantern, electrified for city use, casts a glow over the whole room.

Red energizes this city kitchen, from the deep barn tones of the doors to the brilliant vermilion of five-and-dime bandanas folded as napkins, the kitchen mitts, and the watermelon potholders.

Pear Oatmeal Cake

Makes about 10 servings

1 29-ounce can
  Bartlett pear halves
1 cup quick oats
1/2 cup butter
1 cup firmly packed
  light brown sugar
2 large eggs
1 teaspoon vanilla
  extract
2 cups sifted cake
  flour
1 teaspoon baking
  powder
1 teaspoon baking
  soda
1/4 teaspoon salt
1 teaspoon ground
  cinnamon
1/4 teaspoon ground
  nutmeg
1/2 cup buttermilk
1/3 cup hazelnuts or
  filberts
1/2 cup sugar

1. Drain pears, reserving 1 1/4 cups pear syrup. In small saucepan, heat pear syrup to boiling. Add oats and let stand at room temperature for 20 minutes.

2. In a large bowl with electric mixer, cream butter and brown sugar until light and fluffy. Add eggs, one at a time, beating well after each addition. Beat in vanilla and oatmeal mixture.

3. In small bowl, combine cake flour, baking powder, baking soda, salt, and spices. Heat oven to 350°F.

4. Beat flour mixture alternately with buttermilk into oatmeal-butter mixture. Spread batter evenly in greased and floured 9-inch springform pan.

5. Bake 55 minutes or until cake tests done. Cool in pan on wire rack 10 minutes. Remove from pan; cool on rack completely.

6. Place hazelnuts in a small baking pan; bake 15 minutes in same 350°F oven until golden. Cool and rub off skins; coarsely chop.

7. Just before serving, place cake on serving plate. Cut pear halves lengthwise into halves. Place pear quarters around top of cake layer. Sprinkle with nuts. In small heavy skillet, heat sugar until it melts and turns golden, stirring constantly to dissolve lumps. Remove from heat. Spoon sugar over top of cake. To spin sugar, wave your spoon with melted sugar high over cake to form hard threads.

Country-in-the-City Kitchens

Standard fare in a small urban apartment: the corridor kitchen, closed off at one end and open to a living space at the other. A lucky break here is the big window, which provides an outlook on the skies and weather, and also offers a focal point for hand-sewn curtains and their pretty floral design. The pink in this pattern repeats on the ceiling and walls and again in the checked rag rug and striped dish towels. The drop-leaf table, turned slightly askew on its round rug, can fold down its wings and retire against the wall during buffet dinners or parties. A parasol hides an ugly overhead lighting fixture, while track lighting zeroes in on the work counter and sink area. A little mirror, framed in the same warm wood as used for shelving and countertops, tilts to view whatever is going on in the sink, like an ever-changing theorem painting!

The rich patina of wood and rosy-toned paint makes this kitchen feel expansive and inviting. Rose-petal potpourri gathered in a majolica dish on the table, and in a Shaker-style carrier on the countertop, adds fragrance—a whiff of country, springtime, and romance.

Kitchens in Small Spaces

In country, suburb, and city alike, the kitchen engenders a very homey and warm atmosphere when considered for a tiny space. Coziness is key; and patterns, textures, and colors will reinforce the mood, especially in tandem with well-used and beloved antiques. The busier the textures, in fact, the cheerier the atmosphere!

Awkwardly crammed in under the eaves in a rambling suburban house, this kitchen could have been ignored altogether, but it was revitalized instead. Used as a supplementary cooking space—as there is a bigger kitchen in the house—the little kitchen functions superbly with the minimum of paraphernalia. The wood stove suffices for basic cooking needs, and the sink is located conveniently to serve the dining area. The cabinets, left intact, were scraped down to reveal their original glass panes, and then a new coat of paint was added for a spiffy new look. Wall covering travels up the eaves and over the ceiling to bring the room's many angles into visual alignment, and a fabric was chosen to match. The new curtains made up of this fabric tie back only partway to emphasize their luxurious fullness. To warm up the tile floor, hooked rugs were dropped into place in front of the cabinets and under the table and chairs.

Architecturally, this little kitchen was a hodgepodge, but details maintained their interest. The moldings, for instance, were wide enough to balance favorite paintings, and they continued across the cabinets as cornices.

67

In a one-story Tudor-style cottage built in 1919, all living was compacted into as little space as possible, and the kitchen (left) therefore, was designed merely as an appendage to the dining area. The kitchen, however, was efficient despite its miniscule size, and so modernization was not really necessary. Except for the addition of a combination washer/dryer with a butcher-block top located next to the range, everything remains, including the original cabinets and countertop surrounding the sink. Cosmetic changes were simple and reflected the smallness of scale; the wall covering, for example, displays a sprightly mini-print, and the floorcloth, a checkerboard pattern. The floorcloth, made of canvas and painted, was polyurethaned several times to make it lie flat and also to repel spills. The stool was similarly treated because it is used mainly by small children who want to help out at the sink.

Dining in a corner of the kitchen (right) could have felt claustrophobic in this small New Jersey house, but the tiny area was expanded through the use of a bright red-and-white color scheme. A chair rail divides the wall in half; the lower half was painted white for an airy feeling and to set off the pale pine furnishings. This white extends to the floor, which was cloaked with a marine paint usually applied to decks of boats. Deck paint withstands great abuse because of its thick texture and high gloss. Stenciled clusters of cherries dappled across the floor repeat the pattern in the handmade curtains and window shade. The wall covering, a grid, acts like a "screen" on the walls, making them feel less enclosing. The grid echoes the mullions in the window, leading the eye around the room and on outside.

Opposite: The tiny kitchen plays its patterns off the leaded grid of its single window by building on a checkered motif, on repetitions in the wall-covering pattern, and even on the dishcloth.

Above: Red is the color of energy, and this kitchen sparkles with it, from curtain trim to wallpaper grid to geraniums on a shelf hanging next to the table.

An illustrator who divides his time between the city and the country sought an unpretentious setting for cooking and entertaining—a place where everyone would feel comfortable. Friends all share in the cooking, and so the room had to be big enough to move around in. The farmhouse he found, and its kitchen, were in deplorable condition, but some of the aspects of that state appealed to his sense of beauty—a sense of the immediate and the textural. For example, the old wainscoting, beams, and doors were lovely, and they only needed to be refreshed with paint or varnish. Old linoleum, however, had to go, and it was replaced with narrow planking and warm rag rugs. Collections hang according to whim, with pots and pans and herbs sharing the ceiling with a set of re-webbed chairs snared from a friend's barn. Foods and cats occupy their respective baskets. The wood stove stands away from the walls and can be used for heating water as well as for warmth on nippy days. There are no cupboards in the kitchen, only shelves and tables, so that anything can be reached and used by anyone at any given time. A pantry alongside stashes foods and outdoor gear for gardening. The kitchen, in a way, turns into an ongoing collage, where objects and foods and friends come and go, always easygoing and always with flair.

The focal point of the friendly kitchen is a gigantic circular oak table, which can function in part as an additional work surface, but in the main as the gathering place—up to eight can huddle around it.

Opposite, top: Celadon wares from the 1920s appear as a serene still life on a table near the back door, and their color gently echoes the tonality of the wall paint.

Opposite, bottom: Day-to-day cookware, in cast iron and wood and rattan, rests on wooden slat shelving, which allows air to circulate around the pots and steamers as they dry after wash-up.

Above: Chairs hang up out of the way, yet they can be plucked down readily for dining. The weave of their underseats adds visual texture to the view of the ceiling.

What could be more personal than actually designing and building and finally painting your own kitchen yourself? This particular kitchen in rural Connecticut was lovingly rendered for the sheer pleasure of the task at hand, especially the *trompe l'oeil*—"fool the eye"—paintings adorning everything from cabinets to cupboard to fire screen to dishwasher. The room, though new, featured a miscellany of nooks and awkward jogs which had to be smoothed out visually, if not in fact. The range and refrigerator, located next to each other, fit into separately defined crannies; the tile flooring is repeated behind the range and on the hood so that this junction now appears less austere. The new cabinets, handcrafted after a Welsh prototype, come to a final flourish with an old armoire. The armoire, painted blue, metamorphized into a "coop" with the addition of chickens and eggs painted all around it. Favorite antiques, chosen with an equivalent sense of humor, collect at the dining end of the room. "Firehouse Windsors," chairs that were actually used in firehouses and general stores at the turn of the century, surround the nineteenth-century work table. A Civil War stretcher, which once carried soldiers out of battle, hangs lengthwise from the ceiling as a pot rack, and a butcher's slaughtering platform, now capped with wood block, functions as a work island.

Trompe l'oeil chickens roost with their supply of fresh eggs on every "shelf" of the restored armoire. The armoire houses dinnerware for the adjacent table. A big pig, painted on the front panel of the dishwasher, looks satiated by his load-up duties!

At the heart of country is the love of collecting. Any three objects comprise a collection, but the true collector keeps adding and refining groups or clusters of objects until satisfied. In the country kitchen, collections make a personal statement, declaring to family and friends just what the owners love and care for. When organized imaginatively, collections add graphic appeal to a kitchen, but, more often than not, kitchen collectibles function in harmony with everyday utensils. Bowls and pitchers, pie plates and molds, rolling pins and potato mashers, the list is endless: Kitchen collectibles are noted for their worthiness as utilitarian objects. Many collectibles fall into categories—pottery, woodenware, baskets, metalware, and, lastly, flea-market finds. Some collectibles have escalated in value; others remain bargains. All are loved for what they look like and what they do, and, in this way, add immeasurably to the warmth and charm of the country kitchen.

Country Collections

Pottery

T he tactile qualities of pottery–the heft and bulk of a piece, its glistening glaze, and the contour of its silhouette—are seductive impressions that assure a continued appreciation for this handicraft. Pottery is treasured because of its link to a particular craftsperson, anonymous or well-known, who embellishes his or her work with personal touches—the shaping of the clay in an unexpected manner, the application of a unique glaze, or the signing of individual pieces. Pottery that is mass-produced can affect the collector with equal intensity, though, when ornamentation is derived from a formerly individual perspective or point of view, such as the vision of Canton china as symbolized by a willow tree and bridge over a diminutive stream. Pottery begs to be fondled; made for the hand to hold, it is often used and used again just for the sheer joy of the touch.

The ongoing usefulness of much pottery is proven in this kitchen, where pie plates, pitchers, and bowls always stand ready for serving and storing foods.

Choice plates stand on display throughout the North Carolina house. Some in the kitchen are called "dirt dishes" because of their rugged coloring. The pie plates near the dining table are all unique; each one has a different taper to its sides and a different depth. All pieces are from North Carolina.

Pottery is an integral design element in this North Carolina kitchen (seen on this page and on the preceding page), as it is throughout the house. The house itself, a restored log cabin, was added in order to make room for the kitchen and for the expansion of the pottery collections. The kitchen was sheathed in wide planking for uniformity; the planks were then washed with a sky-blue stain and then rubbed down to dramatize their weathered texture. This color and texture provide the backdrop for the clayware.

The organization of the kitchen, too, allows the pottery to be accommodated everywhere without inhibiting access to the major appliances. Some of the pieces are displayed for viewing only, but most—and especially those in the kitchen—are intended for use on a daily basis. Pots and jugs clustered on the center island, for instance, hold utensils, and pie plates in antique racks stack up to be pulled out for serving foods. For ease of maintenance, a cooktop was selected that has a venting system between the burners. This vent sucks smoke and grease downward and out under the floor, and as a result, the pottery really needs only periodic dusting.

The very utilitarian nature of much pottery is a significant factor in its charm. The chunky form of a milk pitcher—here, many pitchers of indigenous origin are grouped on top of a pie safe—begs to be coddled.

Pottery

Staffordshire Pottery

Specifically catering to an American clientele, over two hundred potteries based in the Staffordshire district in England manufactured distinctive dinnerware with pictorial themes derived from American documents. The cobalt blue transfer that distinguishes this pottery from others made in England was the primary colorway preferred until 1830; other colors, such as pink and brown, were introduced during the decade of the 1840s. Although Staffordshire is still being produced today, few new scenics have been added since the middle of the last century. Favorite motifs included scenes of major events in American history and images of important pieces of architecture, notably university buildings. Borders ran the range from floral patterns to insignias of the new American states to seashells, over a hundred altogether. Some borders identify the manufacturer. Specifically English Staffordshire tends to be paler in coloring than the wares produced for America, which have deep and rich patterns against the white pottery base.

Stoneware

One of the most popular and available collectibles, stoneware was first brought in by settlers from Germany and Flanders, or from England, where adaptations of the German wares were found. American production fired right up, for this utilitarian pottery proved heavy, durable, and chip-proof, perfect for storing liquids and for pickling foods. Formed of a dense clay found in New Jersey and Long Island, most stoneware was fabricated in the Northeast and Midwest. Stoneware is typically gray or tan and is used mainly for crocks, jugs, bottles, and mugs. Before 1850, decoration consisted of an incised naturalistic motif filled with a blue glaze; after that date, when stoneware was produced in great volume, the designs were usually "slipped" or trailed onto the surface of the piece before it was stamped with the name of the pottery manufacturer or purchaser of the piece. The salt glaze that cloaks stoneware was formed by throwing a chunk of rock salt into the kiln. Salt vapors combined chemically with the silica in the stoneware to create the unique glassy coating. A slip, or liquid clay, wash was often applied inside many stoneware pieces, too, to further enhance their durability. Stoneware ceased to be made after about 1910 because technological advances in glass manufacture caused glass vessels to replace stoneware.

Opposite: A collection of Staffordshire pottery is gathered in a step-back cupboard to show off the variety of shapes available for serving use.

Right: The animation of line gives an energetic look to the face of basic utilitarian stoneware crocks.

Redware

Red clay has always been the type most commonly available in the United States, and so the oldest indigenous American pottery was naturally made from this material. Red clay was formed into utilitarian vessels, including plates, bowls, crocks, and jugs; it was also used for bricks and other building materials. Redware, which was very porous, often was coated with a transparent glaze to lend it durability. Designs were simple and direct. Sgraffito patterns incised into the clay body were popular, as were slip patterns, usually made by dribbling liquid yellow clays across the surface. The oldest redware is very deep in tonality, almost brown, as the glaze has aged like a fine vintage wine! Newer redware, especially redware manufactured today, exhibits a brighter, more brilliant hue.

Yellowware

Of all types of pottery produced and used in American homes since the nineteenth century, none is perhaps more utilitarian than yellowware. Fired hard, this buff-colored earthenware, manufactured in great volume in America and in England during the nineteenth century, was formed into many common shapes such as bowls, mugs, and pie plates. Sets of mixing bowls were very popular. Yellowwares exhibit many variations on the yellow hue, from palest mustard to deepest pumpkin. Many yellowware bowls are girdled with white or brown bands, and other pieces, if plain in color, have raised decorations or relief patterns on them. Some yellowwares were sponged in brown or green; these types are usually collected separately. Purely decorative pieces of yellowware crop up rarely; molded animal forms or rolling pins or inkwells appear in the marketplace only now and. then. English yellowwares were typically marked with potter's seal or initials. The value of yellowware, whether English or American, depends both upon the intensity of the color of the piece and the hardness of its glaze.

Opposite: Redware from Pennsylvania is revered for its simplicity and for the dense bronziness of its coloring.

Right: Yellowware comes in so many sizes and shapes it would be difficult to catalog them all, but pie dishes of various sizes, as well as bowls and ramekins, are favorites.

Above: Seaweedlike blotches blur across the bodies of variously shaped mocha ware pieces and harmonize with stripings which girdle these pieces in bands.

Opposite: Deep-toned Rockingham and Bennington wares, grouped together on open shelving, exhibit the density of the mottling so common to both types of pottery.

Mocha Ware

Mocha ware, named for a specific type of decoration which adorns a basic cream or pearl ware pottery of English manufacture, was produced in quantity between 1750 and 1875. Mocha stone was a distinctive English stone that has striations of coloring which the pottery was made to resemble. Because mocha ware was formed of a soft paste clay, the pieces were hollow; this clay was usually formed into mugs and bowls, rarely other shapes. Basic patterns often include bands, either wide or narrow, set in progression at the top and bottom of the piece. These were complemented by seaweed motifs, "earthworm" swirls, orbs called "cat's eyes," and marble and tortoiseshell designs. Against the base cream color, decorations can be found mainly in blue, green, and brown. Very rare pieces of mocha ware display white glaze ornamentation against a dark ground.

Rockingham and Bennington Pottery

The names Rockingham and Bennington, while connoting specific pottery manufacturers, also describe a particular finish that simulates tortoiseshell or marble through the application of a mottled brown glaze to a basic cream body. The prototype for American Rockingham was manufactured in the early nineteenth century in England under the auspices of the Marquis of Rockingham and later by the Leeds pottery works. In America, Rockingham was a coarse pottery produced by every major pottery manufacturer, especially the East Liverpool Pottery Company in Ohio. Bennington pottery was produced by two potteries in Bennington, Vermont, belonging to the Norton and Fenton families. The brown glaze of this pottery is similarly mottled. Bennington pottery often displays the mark of the Nortons or the Fentons, and occasionally both, for the families intermarried.

Slipware

Slip is an extremely wet clay, and slipware is made by dribbling or "trailing" the slip, usually yellow in tonality, continuously through a goose quill over the surface of a basic, often red, earthenware. Long ago, slipware was also decorated with brushes pulling the slip, or even with the fingers. (On stoneware pieces, the designs were executed in oxides of cobalt blue instead of slip yellow or white.)

Slipware plates today are rolled out from balls of clay-like pancakes, and, after the slip design has been trailed across the disc, it is allowed to harden somewhat. The plate is then shaped over a mold and fired with a transparent glaze. The liquid consistency of the slip encourages whimsy in imagery—from animal silhouettes to fanciful calligraphy, from names and words to dots, dashes, and squiggles. Old slipware patterns appear more regular, although loose in design; wavy combed patterns were popular in those days. New slipware is not restricted to plates; mugs, pitchers, ashtrays, and other objects can be found in shops that specialize in contemporary folk art and crafts.

Sponge Ware

The most ardently collected pottery in America today, sponge ware merely describes the open grillwork pattern, on a crude ceramic base, that was probably daubed on with bunched-up fabric swabs. English sponge ware, the prototype for American models, developed out of a tradition of manufacturing spatterware. This pottery exhibited a tight stippled pattern; sponge ware patterns were more open and, although ordered over the surface of the clay, appear looser and lacier. American sponge ware tended to be made from less refined clays than its English antecedent. The colors are more limited than the English too; most American sponge ware is blue and white. Other combinations of colors, which are rarer, are green and white, and a tri-color pattern of brown, green, and ocher. Many sponge patterns may be employed, even on the same piece. American pieces were not marked prior to 1845, and few were signed even thereafter. Most marked pieces came from the International Potteries Company or Ott and Brewer Company. Sponge ware continues to be manufactured today. The zenith of English manufacture was between 1815 and 1830; American potteries reached their peak by 1880.

Opposite: Today's slipware displays more often scribbles than its antique counterpart, where patterns were more densely distributed across the surface of the plate or bowl. Today, slipware can be custom-ordered with personalized sayings, mottoes, or names.

Above: The openwork patterns applied to sponge ware pieces may be randomly scattered over the body of the plate or open vessel, or they may be strictly circumscribed; both types are visible in a collection displayed in a two-door step-back cupboard.

Pottery

Willowware

The Caughley factory in England introduced willowware in about 1780, in response to a desire for Chinese-style porcelain. The blue transfer painting on willowware mimics a Chinese landscape, specifically a bridge spanning a river with willow trees dotting its banks. Later willowware added birds symbolizing the spirits of two lovers fleeing from their irate parents. Because of its enormous popularity, willowware was copied by French and German pottery manufacturers.

A grand collection of willowware fills shelving and cabinetry designed specifically to display it to maximum effect, and the upholstery for twin wing chairs was selected to echo its colors and patterns.

Canton Ware

Canton ware, or Chinese export porcelain, was designed and made specifically in response to orders from the West. Dominated by the British East India Company until the late nineteenth century, this porcelain came to America through England. Canton ware is known for its resilient clay body, which withstands high temperatures—a characteristic much in demand during the nineteenth century, when drinking tea and chocolate was at its zenith. The pottery combined crushed granite, which contained a quartz element, with the local clay; the quartz lends Canton ware its glassy surface texture. Deep cobalt on white provides the coloring for the designs, which were interpreted by Chinese artisans according to Western dictates. All export china was made in the Kiangsi province, in Jingdezhen. When America entered the China trade in 1784, designs began to appear in response to the American market; these included historic and patriotically commemorative patterns as well as the typical Chinese pictorial motifs, which continued in favor. Porcelain had been virtually unknown in Europe until 1708, when Meissen ware was first manufactured; Chinese export porcelain remained, even at that time, less expensive and so was still assured of a continued popularity for many years.

Salt-Glazed Pottery

Salt-glazed pottery is distinguished by a hard, thin coating formed by tossing salt into the kiln at the highest firing temperature. The glaze is similar to a glassy film. Glazes could be colored, but the most popularly collected salt-glazed wares boast characteristically subtle blue-and-white motif. English salt-glazed pottery is often ornamented with an incised decoration. Many American pieces feature relief patterns pressed into the body of the clay. Salt-glazed pieces range from pitchers to mugs—mainly open vessels in various shapes—to containers for cream, sugar, and butter.

Opposite: A salt cellar and sugar tub are two rarer examples of salt-glazed pottery, which was usually fashioned into the mugs and pitchers that were more in demand for kitchen use.

Above: Brand-new Canton china resembles its illustrious antecedent in every detail—including the coloring, which is radiant and rich in its deep tonality.

Right: Each hand-blocked plate by contemporary craftsman Jurg Mark Lanzrein is individually shaped and swirled and then fired, and thus each piece becomes an art object.

Below: A collection of premium pottery is assembled on open shelves in an apartment kitchen; each piece, though similar in motif, was made for a different company. Some pieces are personalized with specific names, not just retail clients.

Pottery Premiums

Quantities of pottery were produced by American factories as premiums, or gifts, which manufacturers and retailers offered with their own products. Ovenware USA and Watt both made wares with an apple motif for a variety of retailers that included supermarkets, oil companies, milk producers, plumbing and heating supply companies, and banks. The apple motif was loosely painted on the basic cream body, and a slogan and the name of the retailer were stenciled on later. Phrases such as "thank you," "compliments of," and "season's greetings" often accompanied the name. The apple-emblazoned wares were primarily distributed during the 1950s and on into the 1960s in the Midwest, specifically in Iowa, Wisconsin, and North Dakota. Many shapes were available, from cookie jars to mugs to bowls to cake plates.

Contemporary Hand-Blocked Pottery

The American crafts movement strongly reinforces the folk arts that have endured for generations, even centuries. This particular plate is just one example of the many kinds of pottery available throughout the United States that are compatible with a country decor. Potter Jurg Mark Lanzrein rolls out different clay bodies in different colors; then he hand-blocks them by pressing them between a piece of canvas and a mold to create the shape of the plate. The linen-textured plate is then fired in the kiln with a transparent glaze to bring out the brilliance of the colors he fuses together. Each and every plate is unique.

Majolica

The decorative and whimsical pottery known as majolica, which is linked with Italian manufacture of the seventeenth and eighteenth centuries, is actually copied from an earlier, more porous, and poorly crafted pottery. Originally an earthenware coated with tin oxide glazes, majolica developed into a pottery known for its lustrous and colorful lead-based glazes. Majolica was also made in Spain, Portugal, and in France, where it was sometimes known as faience. The pieces that collectors today associate with the term derive their forms from the naturalistic shapes devised by Bernard Palissy in France; Palissy experimented with Italian glazes and decided to try out seashell, snail, and other marine-inspired shapes to capture and display those glazes more effectively. Majolica was widely copied in England and America, with leaf forms and images predominating—especially the begonia and the oak. Although majolica was formed in molds, each piece differs, which makes it virtually impossible to identify an individual potter unless a particular piece is marked. Majolica includes plates, platters, and pitchers, but rarely bowls. Colors tend to the bright pastels and jewel tones such as pink, green, and turquoise. English examples of the shell are often edged in yellow or alternating yellow and coral, and some English pieces incorporate serpents into the form.

Overleaf: The fantasy of majolica comes brilliantly to life when many pieces are clustered together. Leaf and animal shapes, and the myriad colors that enhance them, fuse together into one magical collection.

Metalware

An ongoing and consuming passion for graniteware inspired both the color scheme and the basic layout of this kitchen, located in Washington State. First, and obviously, the collection is huge; but another major focal point is the grand classic Universal wood stove, which was bought about twenty years ago for just seventy-five dollars. The stove was refurbished on the outside to show off its brilliant blue finish, which is perfectly compatible with the blue-and-white graniteware. Other appliances stand off to the side of the room, but they relate immediately to the butcher block close at hand. Small appliances hide behind the rolltop in an oak cabinet custom-made just for this purpose. The color cue is carried forth in the sweep of resilient flooring, patterned after ceramic tiles, and also in the mini-checked wall covering next door in the dining area. So that the shapes of the various pieces of graniteware would be displayed properly, the walls of the kitchen were sheathed in a cedar indigenous to this region and stained a neutral gray.

The graniteware collection was assembled over the last quarter-century and is noteworthy for its variety: dinnerware sets (plates, mugs, cups, bowls, and spoons), roasters and fryers, casseroles and molds, colanders and coffeepots—little is omitted.

Graniteware

On a 1930s gas cookstove recently converted to burn wood, a Cape Cod blacksmith and his wife assembled a carefree amalgam of basic gray graniteware. These lowly pieces, manufactured in volume during the latter half of the nineteenth century, prove both serviceable (all pieces can be used for cooking or serving) and a source of comfort and inspiration: The blacksmith now plies a dual trade, as a tinsmith too. Graniteware, made of sheet iron coated with a double layer of porcelain, came in this gray as well as blue and other primary colors. The color was speckled, dribbled, or rippled onto the white undercoat; the double layer gave the pieces greater body and strength. Today, though, any chips are taken in stride by collectors as sure indication that the pieces were used with gusto!

Tinware

Tinware has been a standby in the kitchen since the early eighteenth century. First imported from England, tin was soon crafted in the United States, primarily in Connecticut. Tinsmiths plied their trade as families, with women involved mainly in the design and decoration of specific pieces. Tinware was created from sheet metal—actual tinplate, or sheet iron or steel that had been coated with tin. Early pieces were undecorated, but later tinware was varnished and ornamented. Much tinware is dark, almost black, like the pieces exhibited on the tea towel here. Tinware proved extremely versatile to work with, resulting in many shapes and forms. Buckets, coffeepots, and watering cans were based on rolling the metal. Trays and muffin tins retained a flatter profile. Molding and pressing the tin allowed for imaginative relief decoration. Snips of tin could be fabricated into scoops and ladles, as well as cookie cutters. Some tinware pieces were pierced for use as scrapers; and pierced sheets of tin also adorned doors to pie safes and other kitchen furnishings while allowing air to circulate to foods within.

Opposite: **Although many collectors prefer blue, graniteware in gray is actually a more prevalent variety, and it looks right at home with kitchen decors in many colors.**
Above: **Tinware, or its aluminum counterpart, is still in production today and is as popular as ever with cooks who prefer lightweight, easy-to-heat vessels for cooking.**

Painted Tinware

Painted tinware, often identified as tole, is one of the more colorful collectibles eagerly sought after today. The term *tole* actually describes an early French ironware that was often decorated. Although the earliest tinwares made in the United States were not decorated, by the early part of the nineteenth century socalled japanning had become popular. The japanned finish was a special varnish that protected the tin—or sheet iron or steel—and it demonstrated a high luster simulating the lacquer associated with imported Japanese lacquered wood. The varnished tinware was then dried in a kiln, where the temperature affected its coloration, turning the varnish to a honey tone, or brownish, or black. Decorations came into evidence around 1810 and were usually free-form in design, incorporating floral or fruit motifs, and sometimes borders or bands, depending upon the particular artist or shop where the tinware was produced. Certain artists in Connecticut, Maine, New York State, and Pennsylvania have been positively identified, adding to the value of their work. As with plain tinwares, painted wares come in many forms—from trays, boxes, and caddies to eyeglass cases and candlesticks.

The patterns of painted tinwares, assembled here on shelves, reflect the exuberance of each individual artist.

Crusty Baked Apples

A simple baked apple, topped with applejack-flavored whipped cream, can provide a wonderful finale for a hearty fall dinner such as beef stew. For something a little fancier, try this version in crust.

Makes 8 servings

8 large, firm, tart	*recipe, page 111)*
cooking apples	*1 large egg*
Lemon juice	*beaten with 1*
Apple fillings (recipes	*tablespoon water*
follow page 111)	*About 2 tablespoons*
Sweet pastry (see	*sugar (optional)*

1. Heat oven to 375°F. Core apples, removing a section about 1 1/4 inches in diameter. Peel apples about 1/3 of the way down and rub exposed surface with lemon juice. Fill with one or more fillings.

2. Roll dough out about 1/8 inch thick and cut in 8 squares to fit (almost) around the apples. Depending upon shape, a 3-inch-diameter apple can be covered with a 5- to 5 1/2-inch square of dough.

3. Place dough squares over the fruit and stretch just slightly to fit around and under the bottom. Seal edges underneath and trim off any excess dough with kitchen shears. Cut out decorative leaves and stems from the dough scraps and stick on tops of apples with a little water.

4. Place apples in a shallow baking dish and brush with the egg mixture. Sprinkle liberally with sugar. Bake about 30 minutes until pastry is brown and apples are tender.

Note: For a slightly different effect with less effort, substitute 1 pound frozen puff pastry for the sweet pastry. Roll pastry out slightly thinner than 1/8 inch.

Metalware

Pewter

A canted-top New England step-back cupboard harbors a handsome group of pewter plates, chargers, and measures belonging to a collector in Oklahoma. The pieces, of English and American origin, exhibit the bright luster associated with better-quality pewter, which contains a high proportion of tin to lead or other metals. Pewter wares are classified, defined, and dated partially according to what they copied. Although examples of American pewter exist from the late seventeenth century, the "eight-inch-plate" era, with many undecorated wide-brimmed plates, fell between 1750 and 1825. Before 1800, much pewter was imported, and American examples were based on English models and standards. The "coffeepot" era, from 1825 to 1850, witnessed more sophisticated shapes and forms which mocked the expensive silverware of the period. Pewter from both periods, if marked at all, was marked on the bottom, and in America, almost always with names and letters, not with symbols, which were used abroad. Tankards, pitchers, measures, and beakers were common forms popularized in the colonies. Sadware pieces, named for their heaviness, were usually plates and trenchers hammered or pressed from single sheets of metal.

Pewter is such a soft metal that it is best to simply admire it from afar; its lead content, too, can be hazardous when it comes in contact with many foods.

Metalware

Open-Hearth Utensils

Cooking over the open fire in a big walk-in fireplace spawned a wealth of kitchen utensils, primarily made from wrought iron. Wrought iron was durable and versatile; blacksmiths produced quantities of these utensils as a sideline to their trade in horseshoeing and other major commissions. Objects ranged from simple picks and skewers to complicated braziers, which acted like portable stoves, for bringing hot foods directly to the table. Foods needed to be poked or prodded, turned, skimmed, stirred, or ladled; utensils, therefore, were decreed by these functions. Collectors may easily find forks and skewers, spits and turners, skimmers and ladles. Peels, which resemble flat shovels, were used to pull baked goods from the beehive oven; salamanders, which looked like peels, were used when red-hot, to aid in browning meats by being pressed against the meat as it cooked. Actual shovels were handy for removing ashes from the firebed.

Pots and pans abounded in colonial times. Spiders, named for their skinny legs, acted like skillets but lifted the food above the hot coals. Dutch ovens resembled spiders but boasted lids for steaming or braising foods under cover. Roasters, toasters, and broilers had openwork patterns so that the meats, cheeses, or breads they held would brown properly. For safe transport of hot pots, blacksmiths devised pot lifters, pot pushers, and pot stands, including the trivet. Holders for storing utensils were common, including racks, and these often hung right in the cavity of the fireplace, where a particular utensil could be plucked from the fireplace while cooking was underway. Because the earliest wrought-iron utensils were all hand-forged, they exhibit markings of the hammer; later pieces—especially cook pots and teakettles—were cast or molded.

Baked Apple Fillings

Amounts given per apple:
1 tablespoon soaked raisins mixed with 1 tablespoon orange marmalade

1 tablespoon mixed chopped nuts and raisins mixed with 1 tablespoon cream cheese

Sweet Pastry

Makes one 10-inch tart, 8 to 10 crusty baked apples
2 1/3 cups flour
1 3/4 sticks sweet butter (6 ounces)

A few grains salt
3 tablespoons sugar
2 egg yolks beaten with 4 tablespoons ice water

1. Place flour in mixing bowl and cut in butter quickly with a pastry blender or hands until the mixture resembles very coarse crumbs. With a fork, stir in the salt and sugar. Add yolk mixture a little at a time, stirring with a fork after each addition. (Up to 1 tablespoon additional ice water may be added if necessary.)

2. Press dough gently into a ball and turn onto a floured pastry board. Knead quickly using the heel of your hand to press small bits of dough outward from the ball. Reform ball, wrap and chill 20 minutes or more. Roll dough 1/8 inch thick to a size slightly larger than the pan. Scraps may be used for other purposes immediately or frozen for future use.

A cross section of utensils handcrafted from iron stands at the ready in an open hearth. Open-hearth cookery is steadily gaining in favor once again, as cooks revive colonial recipes for today's fare.

Cast-Iron Trivets

The oldest trivets were hand-forged by blacksmiths to be used for supporting the kettle or cookpot directly over glowing coals and ashes in the open fire. Usually three-legged, trivets exhibited a wide variety of shapes, the most common being circles, triangles, and hearts. Later trivets mimicked the shape of the flatiron, as trivets were logical rests for these particular implements after they were heated. When stoves replaced the open hearth for cooking, trivets were still made—but for supporting hot pots on the table or counter. Many trivets were designed to be admired, too, and were carefully hung on the wall. Fanciful patterns, including floral motifs and dates, filled in the basic silhouette. One favorite shape was the "cathedral," which resembled a gothic arch and was endowed with plenty of fine filigree. Although iron trivets were most commonly used, trivets made of other materials can be found, such as glass, china, and tile.

Cast-Iron Kettles and Pots

Boiling water was a constant necessity in the colonial household, for cooking and for making dyes; for cleaning utensils, dinnerware, and clothing; for healing; and for simple heating. The teakettle, therefore, was always full of boiling water, replenished continuously to ensure a supply. Pots, too, were ubiquitous; these bulbous vessels were used for soups and stews, their sizes varying from the small posnet to the very large cauldron. Kettles had straighter sides. Teakettles were, again, rounded.

Eighteenth-century kettles and pots were manufactured by pouring molten iron into a mold. Side rings and handles were attached to the vessels, and lids made to fit. Pots, kettles, and teakettles were often accompanied by their own specific cooking aids, such as tilters and hooks. Cast-iron teakettles were strictly for kitchen use; better metals, such as copper, were preferred for serving tea in the parlor.

Care of Cast-Iron Ware
Seasoning

Rust, discolored food, a blackened dish towel, and a metallic taste are indications that an old pot or pan needs reseasoning. Always season new iron cookware before using.

1. Scour inside with steel wool or metal scouring pad.
2. Wash with hot, soapy water and dry thoroughly.
3. Coat inside of pan with vegetable oil, shortening, or suet and place in oven set at 300°F for two hours.
4. Remove pan from oven and wipe out fat. Pan is now seasoned.

Cleaning and Storing

● If pan is properly seasoned, it should only need to be wiped clean after use or, at most, quickly washed in hot, soapy water. Dry as well as possible and place over a gas burner briefly or in a warm oven to complete drying.
● Never put away a seasoned pan until it is thoroughly dry, or it will rust.
● Store in a warm, dry place.

Opposite, top: Favored heart motifs occur in many examples of the trivet, especially when worked into the triangular or flatiron silhouette; such trivets were meant to hang on the wall as well as be used.

Opposite, bottom: Teakettles were molded in many sizes; often the largest ones were used in public places such as taverns and taprooms.

Metalware

Muffin Irons

Of all cast-iron cookware, the baking and frying pieces best indicate an increased awareness of cooking techniques and a love for presentation. The many shapes of muffin irons, for example, show that not only plain muffins, but cornsticks, pancakes and tiny breads of every variety can snuggle neatly in their compartments, to be served right from the pan.

Muffin irons surround an all-new brick oven which boasts a heavy and ornately decorated cast-iron door.

Metalware

Copper Utensils

Copper retains and disperses heat so evenly that utensils made of this metal have been coveted by collectors of cookware for generations. Old copper utensils, hand-hammered in England or in the Normandy region of France, often have porcelain or brass handles, which add distinction to their robust and rosy profile. The most sought-after utensils include saucepans of every size, stockpots, gratins, and bowls especially crafted to be used to beat egg whites.

Prized copper saucepans glow on a range hood; the saucepans are antique, and the various molds newly made. Copper bends so easily that molds are an effective way to show off this brilliant metal.

ntique kitchenware crafted from wood goes by the name treen, which literally means "from trees." Treen included bowls and plates—or trenchers—as well as other basic utensils. Treen was initially simple and robust; barrels and other vessels were carved or hollowed out directly from logs. Many families made their own treen. Later, coopers and turners produced woodenware; the coopers' utensils were based on barrel forms and the turners', on pieces that could be turned on a lathe. Colonists preferred the more durable hardwoods for treen—woods such as maple, hickory, and butternut—especially as the earliest woodenware also served for cooking and had to withstand heat and flame. When colonists used trenchers, they would serve dinner on one side of the plate and then flip it over for dessert. When iron, pewter, and ceramics gained favor, many woodenware pieces that had been used primarily for eating disappeared.

In this kitchen in Illinois, woodenware abounds. The owners of the kitchen decided to leave the walls bare of paint so that the honey-colored glow of the planking would remain to complement their collections. The beams, too, were exposed, and these hold just a few of their baskets—over a hundred baskets hang throughout the house. Cupboards and a pie safe stand in for standard cabinets in order to liberate the walls for display purposes. On the walls hang springerle molds, the largest collection in the United States. Springerle are a traditional anise-flavored cookie of German origin. The carvings in the molds are very delicate and often rather whimsical in mood.

Instead of an island, the kitchen is anchored by a kitchen table which is used both for the preparation of foods and for showing off some of the finer pieces of woodenware and salt-glazed pottery; the table proves a handy serving counter, too, for family breakfasts.

The woodenware collected in the kitchen hangs from every conceivable place—rolling pins march down a wall; spingerle molds cluster nearby; mashers and mallets assemble in a corner of the room, hanging from a single beam. Additional finds include an eight-drawer spice cabinet next to the window and a sign just over the same window.

Pantry Boxes

Storing foods from season to season and on throughout the year was a prime concern in early kitchens because of spoilage and insects. To protect foods used daily, various types of boxes were contrived. The most popular containers were constructed in oval or circular shapes, and they often nested or stacked. Their seams were straight and nailed, or were lapped, and often the boxes were painted or even sponged or grained for a textural effect. Woods commonly used for pantry boxes included pine, ash, and beech. In the latter part of the nineteenth century, factories turned out these graduated sets of boxes in quantity, often based on a Shaker style which was a simple oval or round and always lapped in construction.

Bucket Forms

Early woodenware examples were crafted by coopers or turners. Coopers designed and made kitchenware based on the basic barrel shape: butter churns, butter tubs, firkins, piggins (which had one longer stave that could hang on a nail or be used as a handle), and measures. Some of these were very tightly crafted to hold liquids; others were made to contain dry goods such as grains. Many of the early barrel shapes were held together by saplings twisted and entwined around their girth; later barrels were made with iron bands.

Opposite: A tall stack of pantry boxes is a focal point in a dining room; each color complements the next, up the stack.
Above: Early bucket forms adapted to many uses, from holding butter to carrying milk; when they are grouped together, their rough textures offset each other, and differences can be noted in construction.

Woodenware

Burl

When the colonists wanted to create particularly durable bowls or scoops, they sought out the hardwood knots that fester and grow like tumors on the trunks of trees, especially the growths located near the thick base of the tree. These tumors, known today as burls, are harder than the wood they grow on because of the configuration of their whorls and grains. Burl bowls and scoops were formed by adhering as much as possible to the natural curve of the tumor; the cavity was burned, or hollowed out with an adz, and then the bowl or scoop was chiseled smooth. Burl was handcrafted prior to 1750, and often turned on the lathe after that date. Burl is prized today because of its rarity and because of the gentle flow of the grain. Later burl sported carved handles.

All the eccentricities of burl—the dip of the cavity and the undulation of the edge especially—come alive when several bowls are brought together with companion scoops on a tabletop.

Woodenware

Kitchen Utensils

The American infatuation with gadgets gave birth to an immense variety of kitchen tools. First crafted of wood, before the advent of ironworking and tin-smithing, many pieces were highly specialized, contrived to be compatible with a particular food and its preparation. Many of these utensils continued to be made even after iron and tin took over, and they are still produced today. Such tools as rolling pins, potato mashers, apple parers, meat tenderizers, graters, slicers, and paddles are comforting to use and speak of kitchen techniques that were direct and to the point.

Recipes were not complicated, as food was supposed to satisfy hearty appetites first and foremost, and the utensils reflected this honest appreciation of a good meal, prepared well and eaten with gusto. Many wooden utensils are still reasonably priced for the collector and are easily found at flea markets and country fairs as well as in antique shops. One specific item, such as the rolling pin, can be fun to collect for the differentiations in its basic form: fat or narrow, long or short, handled or not. Grouped together, a collection of a single item such as this looks highly sculptural too.

The sculptural quality of wooden utensils livens up a wall and a bin in two country kitchens. Grouping examples of a single item, such as the rolling pin, surprises the collector because of the great variety of forms possible in this simple utilitarian object. Many shapes, conversely—rolling pins combined with mashers and slicers—dramatize the functionality of each piece.

The first American baskets were made by the Indians. Early colonists, recognizing their superb craftsmanship, adapted Indian methods, materials, and forms to their own creations. Baskets always have served a wide variety of purposes and were designed with specific tasks in mind. Those used for carrying foods and grains were woven in the shape most suitable to a particular food. Egg baskets had rounded bases; corn baskets were oblong; potato baskets were bulkier in their shape; and berry baskets were delicate. Openwork baskets for making cheese, drying tobacco, or sifting grains had flat bottoms and shallow sides or rims. Tiny baskets to be hung on the wall had high backs for stability.

Baskets could be woven of almost any resilient grass, reed, or twig; typically, though, they were made from splints pulled away from the trunks of trees, with ash and willow being popular and easy woods to plait. Grasses and reeds were often braided or coiled and then joined together in fat bands, coil to coil. The handles of baskets were often set stiffly, but when required, they could be rendered to permit them to drop down out of the way.

The most common, and trustworthy, place to display baskets is from exposed beams. The baskets hang out of the way and can be admired from every angle. Their shapes, weaves, and handles all stand out, including the construction of their bases. Nantucket baskets have wooden bottoms.

Baskets

The Shakers, practical and persistent in their ardent pursuit of quality, created baskets that are in great demand today. Their baskets were formed on molds using very thin splints; a tight weave distinguishes their construction, as do particular shapes, such as the cat- and kitten-ear bases. Another basket, unique to Nantucket Island, is the lightship basket, which is also formed on a mold. These baskets are similar to Shaker baskets in their meticulous weave, but they have flat wooden bottoms. The oldest Nantucket baskets were woven of rattan brought back from the Orient at the height of the whaling trade. The best examples of the lightship baskets come fitted one inside the other.

Because of the vigorous interplay of horizontals and verticals in any basket weave, it only takes a few baskets to bring dramatic impact to any kitchen. Long hooks work well for hanging baskets from beams because they allow handles to rest loosely and not be bent or twisted against the beam.

Many collectors—and dealers too—become initiated into the fine art of acquisition, and into their knowledge of antiques, through scouring flea markets and attending country auctions. A mere infatuation develops into an all-consuming passion, and the race is on to find the perfect odds and ends to round out a collection. One way to train the eye is to seek out kitchen utensils and accessories, all still reasonable in price and not difficult to find. These purchases can then lead to more ample, or to more particularized collections.

In a simple and spare farmhouse in western Massachusetts, kitchenwares dating from the 1930s and 1940s have found their niche. These particular collectibles have been coming into their own gradually as the interest in Art Deco has burgeoned. Virtually a standby at flea markets, and often ignored by the more industrious collector, these kitchenwares could be found for literally pennies. Many, too, came directly from a grandmother's attic or kitchen, nostalgic reminders of beloved relatives not yet distanced by time.

The owner of this kitchen, though, preferred these wares for their voluptuous shapes, bright colors, and graphics, and began hoarding pieces as he grew to know the flea markets in his region. To show them off, he converted his kitchen from a warren of tiny rooms—a dining room, pantry, and cooking space—into one big, comfortable place for both cooking and entertaining.

All the collectibles in the kitchen are used constantly, except for the salt and peppers gathered on top of the restaurant stove just for graphic display.

Above: Massive quantities of straightforward china were produced in the 1920s and 1930s in response to an overwhelming demand for inexpensive utilitarian dinnerware for kitchens, restaurants, and other settings where food was served. Bright patterns with a geometric bent were often used to set off the basic shape; bright overall colors were used frequently too, as in Fiestaware and Hall's China.

Opposite, top: Depression glass was made to be given away at the movies, or was sold for mere pennies during the lowest ebb of the 1930s. Produced in bulk from the 1920s through the 1940s, Depression glass was fabricated by many of the major glass producers in the Midwest. Colors were cheerful; wares displayed many patterns, from incisions to swirls. Lemonade sets were especially popular, and one favorite color was "golden glow," or amber.

Opposite, bottom: Hall's China was started in Ohio by Robert T. Hall in 1908. Hall contrived many shapes, which he gave fanciful names responsive to the new technology of the times, such as Airflow and Windshield. Many pieces were made for use as premiums or giveaways to induce customers to make major purchases—for a refrigerator, for example. Hall teapots are especially popular today, particularly in bright red and in sky blue.

Filling every available surface, nook, and cranny seems to go hand in hand with the thrill of unearthing and acquiring treasures at the flea market. The walls in a Victorian kitchen in Connecticut reveal an insatiable urge—to fill the walls with tin utensils and cookie cutters. Sieves and strainers, miniature molds and spoons, muffin tins and vegetable peelers—nothing evades the owners' pickings! The patterns these utensils make on the walls are dramatic and humorous in their juxtapositions. And no single find cost more than a few dollars, not even the copper pans which had gone unnoticed in a booth at a Sunday fair.

In a blue-and-white kitchen in rural New Jersey, new and old things mix unexpectedly but without pretension on walls and beams. Once again, the owners—like many collectors—travel off to flea markets at a moment's notice, often on a weekly basis, and they never return home empty-handed. Thus the kitchen changes constantly to accommodate new purchases—baskets, tinware, homespun, graniteware, or whatever. It all goes together because of the blue-and-white theme mixed with natural textures and metals. And everything can be used daily without worry because it cost so little and was used before.

Above: No object has a specific landing place in this kitchen, and so things can be moved around at will and still look at home.

Opposite: Small metalware with open silhouettes keep the walls looking airy even when covered with them all the way to the ceiling. Their patterns also complement the busy design of the tile inset of the floor.

Advertising Tins

Almost as soon as a product was manufactured in America, it was accompanied by its own advertisement. Advertising tins, usually shaped like boxes or bins for convenient storage of the contents within, were a prevalent commodity and became the vehicle for artistic ingenuity in getting the commercial "message" across to the potential consumer. Some graphics were simple, with austere typography, but many a tin displayed tantalizing scenic pictures, beautiful ladies, lovely floral motifs, or other enticing images mated with cleverly intertwined lettering. Most tins were lithographed; rarer ones were stenciled; and rarest to discover are tins with paper labels. (Labels, unless they are meticulously preserved, decompose and vanish.)

Old and new tins happily merge on the collector's shelves today, for many of the newer designs are recapturing the look of their antecedents. Some favorite tins include the bold Lucky Strike tobacco tins with their distinctive green background, and the Cracker Jack tins with the Cracker Jack boy. A collector can choose his or her own brand and turn that brand into a treasure to hunt down at every opportunity!

Today's Grocery Tins

The discerning shopper can turn a pantry full of groceries into an eye-catching collection. Tin cans and paper boxes, when grouped in multiples and gathered according to the color and design of their labels, make a brilliant and graphic statement on open shelving. The backdrop that showcases groceries can remain plain or be patterned with a vivid wall covering to offset the vitality of the designs on the packaged goods. Mixing homemade preserves in jars with the grocery items adds to the visual interest.

Above: Every product available today has an artistic appeal, if treated as such. Setting boxes and tins neatly in rows and stacks, with labels facing front and center, assures their visual dynamics.

Opposite: Tins can be grouped according to color or design, or with the old separate from the new. When mixed all together, they set up a medley of images even if the products—from tobacco to candy—are radically dissimilar.

Homespun Fabrics

The serviceable linen or cotton textiles known as homespuns are associated with many uses, from toweling to clothing to linens appropriate for bed, bath, or kitchen. Typically checked or plaid, homespuns—woven by hand during the period leading up to the Industrial Revolution—were usually yarn dyed with indigo, which was readily available in soluble cubes. Other colors, such as brown and red, are uncommon, for the dyeing methods for these colors were difficult. Red homespuns usually date from the mid-nineteenth century, when factory dyeing and spinning came into being. Linen was the fiber of choice, as flax grew easily in the colonies; cotton, by contrast, was an expensive import until after the invention of the cotton gin in 1793. After that time, cotton began to be produced widely, especially in the South, and the later factory-made textiles were commonly woven of this material. Most handwoven goods do not exceed 40 inches in width, a comfortable width for the handloom, although both hand- and factory-woven textiles might be run narrower. Collections of tea towels and aprons show the variety of patterns that developed from a basic plaid, and how blue-and-white combinations can result in many shades.

Opposite and left: Dowels and pegs afford homespuns their correct vantage point, for textures and colors can be readily seen and appreciated.

Cookie Cutters

Leftover tin scraps, which might have been cast aside by the itinerant or home-based tinsmith, were often salvaged for small wares such as cookie cutters. Bent, pressed, and soldered to form myriad shapes, from straightforward rounds and hearts to fanciful animals, cookie cutters have been enjoyed by countless generations of young and old alike, for sugar-and-butter cookies are a true staple of American cooking. When cookie cutters join together on a wall, they add an element of whimsy to any kitchen; they may also be gathered in a basket or bin, to be pulled out anytime cookie making is in the offing. Old cookie cutters are distinguished by soldering marks at the seams and by their tin backings, which flare out beyond the edges of the actual tin cookie-cutter shape.

Animals

Animals of every description strike the fancy of many a collector, enhancing both the traditional country decor and the urban setting—for animals are humorous as well as appealing. This particular herd of cattle is just one such collection; sheep, pigs, geese, ducks, and other barnyard beasts also curry favor. Toys, a highly prized collectible in their own right, amplify an animal grouping; pull toys, here true in detail to their bucolic counterparts, roam below a series of pastoral paintings.

Cookie cutters, big and small, show how adaptable a simple sugar-cookie recipe could be. Rolling out dough was one operation; cutting the cookies could vary considerably depending upon the cutter shapes.

Clustering a specific collection—such as cows—without distraction, offers a singular viewpoint that would not be as evident if the collection were scattered around the room.

S etting the table is at once a gesture of welcome and an invitation to dine. The opportunity for expressing yourself through the presentation of foods is limited only by your imagination, for every object that comes to the table can speak in your voice, telling family and guests how much you enjoy having them join you for this meal. Country tables may be informal, utilizing simple objects in conjunction with basic tablewares such as ironstone and jelly glasses. Or the table may present a more cluttered display, bringing fruits and flowers of the season to harmonize with favorite collectibles, filling the table from corner to corner. Whether bounteous or plain, the country table feels casual, enjoining all comers to linger and savor every morsel and every moment.

Setting the Country Table

When the atmosphere is casual, a meal instantaneously converts all guests into friends; informality appeals to all generations, and dining becomes a truly family-style experience. When there's little or no reliance on ceremony, anyone and everyone can comfortably drop in on the fun.

Combinations of traditional and unexpected furnishings and accessories enliven many a country decor. In an antique dealer's house in Illinois, a robust and amusing parade of roosters—the owner's prime collectible—struts the length of a two-board harvest table. The roosters—weathervanes, advertising art, chocolate molds, and a candle—galvanize the diners' gaze while simultaneously shielding the table from the adjoining living area. Diners eat at the table informally, lunch-counter-style, from unmatched sponge-decorated plates. Eggs presented in shot glasses and milk poured into ice-cream-soda glasses further the notion that anything goes in a daring yet congenial mix of tablewares.

Each of the sponge-ware plates on the honey-hued harvest table boasts a different motif, including a bird, a star, and a flower.

Harvest Pumpkin Soup

This creamy soup can be served in a seeded fresh pumpkin or in soup bowls.

Makes 6 cups, or about 6 to 8 servings

2 tablespoons butter or margarine	2 cups fresh pumpkin purée
1 large onion, chopped	1/2 teaspoon salt
1 large potato, pared and diced	1/4 teaspoon ground nutmeg
3 cups homemade or canned chicken broth	1/8 teaspoon white pepper
1 16-ounce can pumpkin or	1/2 pint heavy or whipping cream
	Packaged croutons

1. In 3-quart saucepan over medium heat, in hot butter or margarine, cook onion and potato 5 minutes, stirring occasionally. Add chicken broth; heat to boiling. Cover and cook over low heat until the vegetables are tender.

2. Ladle half of the vegetable mixture into the container of an electric blender. Cover and blend until smooth. Add remaining mixture and blend until smooth. Return to the saucepan.

3. Add pumpkin, salt, nutmeg, and pepper. Over high heat, heat to boiling. Cover. Reduce heat to low; cook 10 minutes. Stir in cream; heat through.

4. To serve, ladle into a seeded pumpkin or soup bowls; garnish with croutons.

Easy and Informal

Typically, beach houses offer space at a premium and their furnishings tend to be minimal, and so dining often sets up rather haphazardly in one corner of the basic living space. Dressed with a quilt, however, a formerly disreputable-looking junkyard table assumes a festive air, in anticipation of an intimate dinner. The quilt acts as a graphic backdrop for rustic ironstone dishes. Butter served in a heart-shaped mold, gentle-hued candles, and a pretty bouquet of flowers add to the romantic ambiance.

Caring for Your Quilt

A good credo to follow is, if you love it, use it—and this applies to the use of quilts in many locations throughout the house. Don't hesitate to drape a table with a quilt, but be sure to choose one of less than museum quality, preferably a flea-market find. If you want to cover a table with a truly fine quilt, though, consider having a piece of glass cut the same shape as the top of your table to protect the quilt from soiling. Or layer another fabric, handkerchief-style, over the quilt so that just the sides show. If you enjoy sewing, make your own new quilt from scraps and remnants, just as your ancestors did, in a pattern you like; it is easy to stitch up a quilt on the sewing machine, and you can work with easy-care fabrics if you want to wash the quilt over and over again.

Ironstone can be taken directly from oven to table if desired, although it would be wise to place trivets underneath to protect the quilt from the hot plates.

Blue and white checks, a perennial country favorite, set the design scheme for a porch that was converted into a spacious dining area adjoining the kitchen in an Illinois farmhouse. The wallpaper, a direct copy of an early homespun pattern, juxtaposes with the checked valances, sewn up from upholstery fabric. Place mats and napkins were handmade to match from the same fabric. Seating around a big square table gives everyone plenty of room to talk and to reach serving dishes. Blue graniteware withstands everyday use for hearty family dining, and bright red apples anchor the napkins to the plates as succulent "invitations." The tin silhouettes that romp across the window mullions confirm the barnlike mood, to balance their real-life counterparts in the pastures just outside.

Sew a Runner for the Table

You can quilt a runner to warm up a winter table, or you can sew it up instead in an unadorned flat style to equal effect. Measure the width of your table, subtracting the depth of two place settings opposite one another so that the completed runner can slip between them. To calculate length: Measure the length of the table and add a foot to each end. Cut twin pieces of fabric according to these dimensions, but remember to add on a seam allowance all around before cutting. If you accent the runner with cording, pin the cording around the perimeter of the right side of one piece of the fabric, with the cording turned in, away from the edge and toward the pattern. Pin the companion piece of fabric, face down, to the cording and fabric that faces up. Stitch all around, as if for a pillow case, leaving one end open. Flip inside out so that patterns and cording return to the outside. Stuff the runner "case" with quilt batting, and stitch the stuffed runner along a grid of your choice. Last step: Close the open end of the runner with hand stitching.

Popular blue is apparent everywhere in the room, right down to the overalls on the doll leaning against the miniature rocking horse at the center of the table.

Easy and Informal

Coordinating the table linens with decorator fabrics used at the windows and on seat cushions brings a dining area into sharp focus and further enhances its atmosphere of coziness and warmth. The linens here, all snuggled next to a huge fieldstone fireplace, mix and match within a red-and-green palette. The dinnerware mingles well within this color range; shiny pewterlike "charger" plates brilliantly underscore leafy-green antique majolica and plain white ironstone soup bowls. Cheeses and fruits, ripe for selection, stand as a tantalizing centerpiece and allow everyone to continue the meal in a relaxed fashion, from soup onward, without ever leaving the table!

Old and new dinnerware marries happily on this winter table, as do the checks and flowers on the various linens.

It is not mandatory that a house date from the colonial period in order to have a colonial style. This farmhouse in rural Pennsylvania, for example, appears as if it had been handed down in one family for generations—but it is, in fact, brand-new. The mix of furnishings and accessories also purposefully blends old with new. Therefore, there are no rules here but one: Everything must go together. Antique pottery from France and the United States fills the dining cupboard, but the table is always set with all-new local reproductions, most practical when feeding a large family. Bittersweet and goldenrod, plucked from the roadside, were gathered into a berry basket, their bright colors compatible with dinnerware and decor.

New slipware is distinguished by whimsical animal shapes, which lend a lighthearted note to the already easygoing table.

Drying Herbs

Dried herbs accentuate the beams of many country kitchens. If you grow herbs in your garden, you may want to add a few bunches to your own kitchen decor. Gather herbs of your choice—small-leafed varieties look best, as large-leafed herbs tend to crumble and look messy—in late spring or early summer, when natural oils are most concentrated in the leaves. Pick just after the dew has evaporated on a dry, sunny morning; wet herbs become moldy. Clip with shears for a clean cut, leaving roots and the thickest part of the stem behind to ensure continued growth of the herb. Direct sunlight fades most herbs, and so you should dry yours in a cool, shaded place. Separate the herbs by type, as, once dried, many herbs tend to look alike. Bunch each herb and tie with twine or strong string. Wash each bunch quickly under cold water to remove dust, and then pat dry between paper towels. Air drying should take about two days. Rack drying in a 100°F oven takes just a few minutes. Check the oven frequently; you can keep the oven door open throughout the process. Herbs can hang indefinitely for display purposes, but they lose their taste quickly. If you want to use dried herbs, you have to remove the leaves from the stems and store in jars in a cool, dark place, away from heat and sunlight. Some favorite herbs to dry and hang are thyme, oregano, marjoram, lemon balm, and tarragon.

A bright and cheerful table elicits a reciprocal response from diners, inspiring them to enjoy everything about the meal, from the carefree—albeit careful—presentation of food and drink to the buoyant chatter that involves one and all. The atmosphere is so infectious, that everyone leaves the table in an ebullient mood.

In Ohio, a new house meticulously constructed in a time-honored Early American design was updated in the kitchen with an expansive bay window to let in light and overlook an herb garden. Snugly settled right in the nook created by the bay, a hand-pegged tavern table awaits the serving of morning coffee. To further define this breakfast area and grant it warmth, an Oriental rug was placed beneath the table. The scale of its pattern harmonizes with the mini-check of the gingham valance, and its formality perfectly suits the table setting, which is delicate and refined. A nosegay of tiny flowers and greens, collected in a creamer to match the china, adds color.

The Perfect Cup of Tea

Water for tea should be absolutely fresh, never reboiled. Bring fresh water in your kettle to the boil. Pour boiling water into your teapot, to warm it, and then return this water to the kettle. Measure one teaspoonful of your favorite tea leaves per cup—plus one extra teaspoonful for the pot—into the teapot, and then pour boiling water back into the teapot over the leaves. Let the tea steep for five minutes, and then strain into cups. It is always preferable to dilute tea in the cup, by adding boiling water to the full-strength brewed tea. If you enjoy weak tea, therefore, pour just a little of the brewed tea into your cup, and then add boiling water until the tea is the strength you like. If you take milk with your tea, pour it into the cup prior to adding any tea. Add sugar to sweeten: one lump, or two?

Amid rustic furnishings, the gently curved tea service appears fragile at first glance, but it is actually very strong—and dishwasher-safe besides!

Two tables, unclad and dependent only upon monochromatic white mellowed with accents of garden flowers and greenery, reveal how crisp and clear table settings can be. White china gives the architecture in these rooms full breathing space, without distraction. In a barn, a whole loftlike mezzanine is given over to a huge round table where up to ten people can sit comfortably. Fine porcelain joins chunky ironstone and clouded glass—all in white—and each place is accentuated by a frilly paper doily. In an island getaway, a sturdy pine table welcomes equally hearty ironstone, layered for the first and main courses, with breads and cheeses, tea and berries at the ready for serving.

Opposite: In a barn, landscaping evolves from the table! A furry green bush, bought for the garden, reposes in a grand ironstone serving bowl at the center of the table during dinner, and then is removed for planting.

Above: In an island home, freshly picked garden flowers grace a trio of ironstone pitchers which are artlessly positioned on the table.

Entertaining at its best is always welcoming, and tables that receive their guests with warmth encourage candor and conviviality. No stranger feels at a loss here, but is quickly and effortlessly absorbed into the congenial assembly.

Bold stripings, reminiscent of beach umbrellas, spontaneously spruce up any table, any season of the year. Stripes sparkle and are an especially zesty choice for casual dining and for parties. On a twiggy table, dinnerware sporting bands in bright primary hues teams up with striated mugs and multistriped linens.

Antique Gaudy Dutch and Stickware dinnerwares—which line the shelves of a double-door step-back cupboard in this Connecticut farmhouse—are perfectly enjoyable as a collection, but all pieces emerge when necessary to set the table too. The bright floral patterns on the dishes meet their match in the vivid blue stripes edging the antique jacquard table linens. The linens are used constantly without fear of overuse or wear and tear. If these collections, after all, have lasted this long, why not longer?

Above: For festive occasions, a china with an outgoing personality—striped or banded (or dotted or checked)—adds cheer.

Opposite: On a wide three-board pine table, elements of humor abound: A wasp-waisted wire container holds wooden fruit; two tiny birds peck at the table runner; and a ceramic cow gazes with bucolic contentment from atop a butter tub.

Three one-hundred-year-old log cabins were joined together to create a cozy homestead in Tennessee, and one cabin is devoted purely to cooking and dining. A massive fireplace provides a focal point for the room, and the dining table sits right near it to take advantage of its warmth. Pewterlike goblets and over-scaled plates glow against the raw surface of the pre-1870 Tennessee table; the table has two big drawers that supposedly stored leftovers along with utensils between meals in the olden days.

Food presides in a log-cabin kitchen. Preserves take the place of collections in the corner cupboard; muffins, butter, and apples take the place of a conventional centerpiece on the table.

The lack of pretension and the winning manner of a simply adorned table inspires the affection of all those who come to share the food there. Here, every object assumes a friendly identity, and every food appears natural and good and free of artifice. This type of tablesetting is uninhibited in its appeal, much like a picnic would be.

In California, the country look represents an infatuation with the out-of-doors. In this canyonside home, a 20-foot-high wall of glass allows massive doses of light to flood the combination kitchen/dining room, and trees and plants are continuously rotated to add to the airy and gardenlike feeling. In keeping, too: floors paved with big handmade Mexican tiles and furnishings all of pale pine. The pine pieces come from Scandinavia, Ireland, Canada, and the United States as permanent souvenirs of a love of travel. The table is outfitted with a homespun cloth, hand-thrown pottery, and wooden serving plates, also collected on travels.

The overriding design concern in this country house was comfort at a low cost. The huge table was handmade in less than four hours using lumberyard scraps and then sealed with polyurethane to repel spills. Mats of corrugated rubber also shrug off soil. All plates and glasses can be replaced in a flash, for they are standard fare at any kitchen-supply outlet and can be bought in quantities at rock-bottom prices. Glass, too, defers to the colors and textures of foods and beverages so that any meal—plain or fancy—always looks delicious. Porcelain trivets have holes in them to more effectively divert heat.

Opposite: Pale gray North Carolina pottery stacks atop Swedish pine serving dishes in this unaffected table setting. The single note of artifice is a bandana tied at the throat of the bottle of white wine, in a happy gesture of salute to the forthcoming meal.
Left: The near-invisibility of glass dishes makes them especially versatile in setting the table; they look good with all foods, and they mix well with wood and porcelain.

Pure and Simple

Old graniteware is a prime collectible, but new versions of the old, in vibrant primary tones—as well as black—ensure its enduring appeal. A breakfast-tray set with black graniteware would look just as handsome in the city as in the country, especially due to the fact that black dinnerware is considered sophisticated in urban locales. Because graniteware is unbreakable, it can travel right on out of the house to the park, woods, or beach for a picnic—or even back to the campfire, where some of the earliest pieces started on their road to popularity!

The spaciousness of a big barn was simulated in a newly built dining room by extending the ceiling and adding a loft overlook. The dining area is framed in by beams and is then stabilized by a long, highly polished harvest table set with hand-painted faience from France. The faience, though subtly colored, is ample in shape and form, and so it is not diminished by the size of the room. Flatware, too, feels heavy to the hand, a perfect complement to the earthenware.

Above: Graniteware (paint-over-metal) is a particularly durable type of dinnerware and is immensely popular for casual dining. It also mixes well with china when used as an underliner for other plates or bowls.

Opposite: French earthenware, called faience, is typically painted with figures or pastoral scenes. This particular style displays pretty bird cages instead and is festooned with ribbons and flowers.

No one ever seems to want to vacate a room or leave a table that is cozy in feeling, for everything brought to this place beckons all comers to stay awhile for the sake of friendship. Here, conversation lasts long while coffee mugs or wineglasses are refilled and candles burn down to the quick.

The kitchen in this Massachusetts bungalow is so miniscule that everything has to serve more than one purpose. The jelly cupboard, with its back to the kitchen table, acts as divider, serving surface, and storage cabinet. Kitchenware mixes with dinnerware, even in table setups, to eliminate the need to keep full sets of anything on hand. Thus, spout-lipped mixing bowls step in for soup or cereal bowls, and kitchen towels, an arm's length away at the sink, suffice instead of traditional mats and napkins.

Pictorial motifs and images enhance many styles of country-inspired china, from village scenes to pastoral vignettes, from houses and barns to a full range of barnyard beasts.

Opposite: Dining by candlelight simplifies lighting needs over the table and imparts a romantic aura besides.

Above: On a teacup and saucer, a rosy cow chews on emerald-green grass and dewy flowers, thus evoking her Irish heritage.

All the furnishings in this log cabin in South Carolina were discovered locally, including the three-board table from Edgefield County. A settle bench, draped with a quilt, cozies up to the table to accompany a quartet of rabbit-ear chairs. These chairs were made especially to lean back in! Napkins have been dropped over the backs of the chairs in anticipation of finger-licking Southern fried chicken, johnnycake, and cornbread wedges streaked with butter and honey. Edgefield pottery, noted for its taupe coloring and free-form patterns, stands here and there in the room.

The dishes on the 1840s dining table are actually tin, painted white and banded with blue. The same color of blue is echoed on the cushions that soften the splint seats of the dining chairs.

Christmas is more than just a holiday. Warm wishes abound, and a special spirit of giving imbues every room in the house with feeling. Every sense is indulged: The sparkle of candle flames, fire's glow, and the patterns of gift wraps and trims; traditional carols and madrigals; the aroma of spices and pomanders; the taste of freshly made foods and drinks; and finally, all the spontaneous hugs for family and friends. This is the time to unfold and cook up treasured recipes, unwrap ornaments that have been locked away in the attic over the year, cut down a perfect tree, and light candles in every window. It's a time to bring everyone you love together again.

In an urban townhouse, the table awaits guests who can create their own personal pomanders from all kinds of fruits such as apples, oranges, lemons, and limes, while taking time out to nibble a cookie or two.

Overleaf: A bounteous buffet welcomes all comers to this suburban fireside, from home-smoked turkey to three kinds of cake. Christmas plates emerge from under wraps to honor the occasion. Poinsettias and local greens, red candles, and besprigged linens finalize the scene.

One way to accessorize a holiday table is to present a small favor right in the center of everyone's plate—a tiny collectible, perhaps, or, better yet, an ornament or gift you made yourself. This beeswax bear was formed in a chilled chocolate mold and then tied with ribbon to a bit of greenery. A checked blanket is the backdrop.

An everyday china can be dressed up to greet the holidays with trimmings and special accessories. A bright red chubby dinnerware set looks especially festive with the addition of equally rosy linens tied with ribbons and apple ornaments. A quilt top used as a tablecloth sets up a vivid counterpoint with its energetic pattern in triangles and squares.

Making Beeswax Ornaments

Warm one pound of beeswax with 3.2 ounces of paraffin very slowly, on the lowest setting, in an old electric frypan. (Never heat paraffin over an open flame or on a burner, as it is extremely flammable.) Oil and chill molds of your choice. Ladle a continuous flow of melted wax into the mold until filled. Refrigerate. When cool, release wax figure and trim off excess wax with a paring knife. Remove oil with soapy water and then dry. If you want to hang your beeswax ornaments, pierce them with a hot ice pick and then string with thread or fishing line.

Above: Pewterlike dinnerware, wooden servers underneath, and a cozy blanket all spell warmth, symbolic of the holiday spirit. **Opposite:** Tiny parcels nestle under a boxwood tree to bring a joyful air to a Christmas meal.

Café Brulot

This recipe is traditionally made and served in a chafing dish; it may also be prepared in a skillet and transferred to a small punch bowl.

Makes 8 servings
Zest or peel of one orange
Zest or peel of one lemon
1 short cinnamon stick
6 whole cloves
4 teaspoons sugar
3/4 cup cognac, warmed
1 quart strong, hot coffee

1. In chafing dish, combine orange and lemon peel, cinnamon stick, cloves, sugar, and cognac. Using a long match, ignite cognac. Stir until sugar dissolves.

2. Slowly add coffee; stir well. Serve in demitasse cups.

Champagne Fruit Punch

The fruit is marinated ahead of time, and the champagne is added just before serving.

Makes 20 servings
1 pint strawberries, hulled, and halved or quartered
1 8-ounce can pineapple chunks packed in their own juice
1/4 cup sugar
1/2 cup brandy
2 tablespoons lemon juice
2 750-ml. bottles sauterne

1 750-ml. bottle champagne or sparkling wine, chilled

1. In large bowl, combine strawberries, pineapple chunks with their juice, sugar, brandy, lemon juice, and sauterne. Refrigerate until cold.

2. Pour fruit mixture into punch bowl. Just before serving, add champagne.

Holiday Wassail

Tiny lady apples and clove-studded oranges float in this traditional punch.

Makes 12 servings
6 small oranges
Whole cloves
1 quart apple juice
3 cups light rum
2 cups orange juice
1 12-ounce can apricot nectar
1/8 teaspoon ground ginger
6 lady apples
Cinnamon sticks

1. Heat oven to 350°F. Stud oranges with cloves; place in a shallow baking dish. Bake for 30 minutes.

2. In large saucepan over high heat, heat juices, rum, nectar, and ginger just to boiling.

3. Pour into heat-resistant punch bowl. Add oranges and ap-ples, garnish with cinnamon sticks, and serve.

Festive Cranberry Punch

A non-alcoholic punch for kids—and grown-ups, too. Just mix and serve.

Makes 24 servings
1 32-ounce bottle cranberry juice cocktail, chilled
1 12-ounce can frozen orange juice concentrate, thawed
1 6-ounce can frozen lemonade, thawed
2 liters carbonated lemon-lime soda or seltzer, chilled
Ice cubes

1. In large punch bowl, combine cranberry juice, orange juice, and lemonade.

2. Stir in soda and ice cubes. Serve immediately.

Brunch Punch

When you're expecting a large crowd over for a Christmas brunch, serve this tomato-based drink.

Makes 20 servings
2 46-ounce cans tomato juice, chilled
1 750-ml. bottle light or dark rum

2¹/₂ teaspoons Worcestershire
   sauce
¹/₃ cup lemon or lime juice
Salt or pepper to taste
Ice block
Lemon or lime slices

1. In large punch bowl, combine tomato juice, rum, Worcestershire sauce, lemon juice, and salt and pepper to taste.

2. Add block of ice. Garnish with thinly sliced lemons or limes, if desired.

Coffee-Nog Punch
For a change of pace, try this updated eggnog.
Makes 12 servings
4 large eggs
*1 14-ounce can sweetened
   condensed (not evaporated)
   milk*
3 cups milk
1 tablespoon instant coffee
¹/₂ cup brandy
¹/₃ cup rum cream liqueur
*1 cup heavy or whipping cream,
   whipped*

1. In large bowl with mixer at high speed, beat eggs until frothy. At low speed, beat in sweetened condensed milk, milk, and coffee until coffee dissolves.

2. Beat in brandy and rum cream. Refrigerate until cold.

Pour into punch bowl; top with whipped cream and a dash of ground cinnamon, if desired.

Creamy Eggnog
Serve this full-bodied holiday drink at your next open-house party.

Makes about 24 servings
1 dozen eggs
1¹/₂ cups sugar
1 liter bourbon
1 quart heavy cream
1 quart milk
Ground nutmeg
Whipped cream

1. Separate eggs. In large bowl with mixer at low speed, beat egg yolks and 1 cup sugar until blended. At high speed, beat until thick and lemon-colored. Gradually beat in bourbon. Refrigerate until cold.

2. In punch bowl, combine egg-yolk mixture, cream, and milk. In large bowl with mixer at high speed, beat egg whites until soft peaks form. Gradually beat in remaining ¹/₂ cup sugar until stiff peaks form. With wire whisk, stir egg whites into yolk mixture until mixed. Top with whipped cream and a sprinkle of nutmeg.

Glogg
The recipe for this Swedish wine punch may be varied according to personal taste. Red port may be used instead of red wine, and vodka may be used in place of aquavit.

Makes 10 to 12 servings
*2 750-ml. bottles dry red wine
   (about 7 cups)*
*2 tablespoons finely grated
   orange peel*
1 cup sugar, or to taste
10 cardamom pods, crushed
10 whole cloves
4 short cinnamon sticks
1 750-ml. bottle aquavit
1 cup dark seedless raisins
*¹/₂ cup sliced or whole blanched
   almonds*

1. In large stainless or enamel sauce pot (not aluminum), heat wine, orange peel, sugar, and spices, just until sugar is completely dissolved and mixture is hot. Do not let it boil.

2. Remove from heat. In medium saucepan, heat aquavit just until warm; with long match, ignite aquavit and let it burn down. Pour into wine mixture. Strain into large heat-resistant bowl; add raisins and almonds.

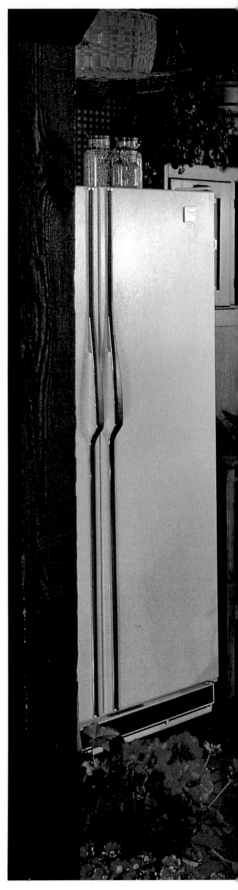

Hub. Heart. Center. These words recur again and again to describe the warm and welcoming country kitchens that we have shown you on the preceding pages. Such kitchens not only tempt you with ideas for decorating and displaying your favorite collections, but also send and receive all the energy of the family day, from breakfast straight on through to bedtime nibbles.

The comfortable country kitchen, then, must not only look wonderful but also work efficiently. The information we have gathered in this chapter has been geared to inspire you to plan your new and improved kitchen so that it will indeed function effectively for you—for cooking, serving, eating and entertaining, and cleanup. A new kitchen will last you fifteen years or more. With careful planning, this room should grow with you and your family, and will encompass many activities in the same space.

Planning the Country Kitchen

To get you started on your dream kitchen, we have drafted a questionnaire that will lead you through the major problem areas and concerns encountered in the kitchen: layout, traffic patterns (moving through the room), appliance choices, storage and countertop space, and lighting. Think of every option and possibility available, and, as you go along, jot down ideas that might be inspired by some of your answers. Share the questionnaire with your whole family, and your friends too, for their opinions count as much as yours. Everyone wants to feel good in this place. A well-designed kitchen is, after all, a happy place, satisfying to one and all. Your kitchen, when perfectly suited to your personal lifestyle, will be a room you will enjoy and everyone will love.

The Cooks

How many members of your family cook?
    Only you
    Your husband/wife
    Children
    Other
Who cooks the most meals?

How tall is the primary cook?
How tall are other cooks in your family?
How many meals do you eat in your kitchen?
    None
    Breakfast
    Mid-morning coffee break or snack
    Lunch
    Mid-afternoon snack
    Supper or dinner
    Late-evening snack
How elaborate is the preparation of each of the above meals or snacks?
    On-the-run
    Prepared from memory
    Prepared from recipes
How many people participate in the preparation of each of the above meals or snacks?

How many of the above meals or snacks does your family eat together?

What is your usual cooking style?
    Meals-in-minutes
    Microwave cookery
    Stockpots, stews, and casseroles
    Grilling, griddle cooking, and roasting
    Wok cooking, stir-frying, and steam cookery
    Ethnic specialties such as Italian, Tex-Mex

Do you do quantity baking?

Do you can and preserve foods?

Entertaining

How often do you entertain?
   Once a week
   More than once a week
   Once a month
   Less often

How many people do you usually entertain on a given occasion?
   Two to six
   Eight to twelve
   A bigger crowd

How would you characterize your entertaining style?
   Formal
   Informal

How often do you entertain in the following manner?
   Sit-down dinners
   Buffets
   Luncheons
   Cocktail parties
   Barbecues

Do you entertain in your kitchen?

Do your children entertain in the kitchen?

Do you like to serve drinks in your kitchen?

Do you enjoy having your guests in the kitchen while you are cooking?

Children

How much time do your children spend in the kitchen?

If they are young, do they play there?

If they are older, do they do their homework there?

Shopping

What are your shopping habits?
   Shop daily
   Shop twice a week
   Shop once a week
   Shop once or twice a month

Do you shop for staples less often and then fill in?

Do you stockpile staples such as paper products, cleaning aids, and major food items?

Do you buy in bulk or in jumbo sizes often?

How much frozen food do you keep on hand?

How many canned goods?

How many condiments and spices?

How many exotic foods?

How many beverages, including canned and bottled goods?

How many paper products?

Do you have to move things around in your cabinets to find what you need?

Can you reach everything you need that you use most often?

Do you always seem to be running out of certain foods, and forget about other foods?

Ask yourself these same questions about your kitchen wares, including accessibility of utensils and pots and pans.

Are your countertops cluttered?

Is there enough counter space to prepare meals as well as serve them and clean up afterward?

Appliances

Which of the following small appliances do you own, and how often do you use each of them?

Questionnaire

Toaster   Toaster/oven   Mixer/blender   Food
   processor
Coffee maker   Juicer/extractor
   Slow cooker   Electric frypan
Ice-cream maker   Yoghurt maker
   Popcorn popper
Meat/vegetable slicer   Meat grinder   Waffle iron
Electric can opener   Electric knife sharpener
   Ice crusher
Hand mixer   Stand mixer

Do you have difficulty locating and using any or all of your small appliances?

Which of the following major appliances would you like to own, upgrade, or replace?
   Range—standard, self-clean, or continuous-clean
      Gas or electric
   Combination range—including microwave or
      convection oven
   Cooktop—standard, or combination unit including
   grill, griddle, or rotisserie attachments and self-vent
      Gas or electric
   Wall ovens—standard pair, or combination unit
      including microwave or convection oven
   Microwave oven—countertop or under-cabinet
   Refrigerator/freezer—side-by-side, over-under, or
      under-over
   Self-defrost
   Standing freezer
   Ice machine
   Trash compactor
   Dishwasher
   Washer and dryer

Do you separate everyday flatware, dinnerware, and glassware from special-occasion tableware?

Do you own bulky or oddly proportioned serving pieces, and how often do you use these?

Ventilation, Lighting, and Noise
Do you have an adequate ventilation system?

Is the lighting adequate for the activities in your kitchen?
   Ambient or overall
   Lighting for dining
   Lighting over countertops
How effective is the sound insulation in your kitchen?
   Is your kitchen too noisy?

Traffic Patterns and Activity Centers
How far away is the working area in your kitchen from the following areas?
   Car and garage
   Mudroom
   Dining room
   Family room
   Pantry
   Laundry
   Patio, terrace, or backyard
How do people usually go through your kitchen?

How many doors lead into the kitchen?

Are the doors conveniently placed?

Do doors open into the work area or away from it?

Can you reroute children to their own rooms without having them pass through the work area?

Do appliance doors open conveniently?

Do appliance doors block the work area?

Can everyone get to the eating area without bothering the cook?

Can everyone using the kitchen table get up and move about without bothering those still seated?

Can people move around the table easily when everyone is seated?

Does the cook have enough room to move around while preparing and serving a meal?

If two or more people cook, do they get in each other's way?

Is the cook (or cooks) moving around too much during even the simplest tasks, such as making a cup of coffee?

Is there enough room for friends to gather and talk with the cook during the preparation of a meal or snack?

Is there a place for children to play, do homework, or sit and talk while the cook is working?

How often do you use electronics in your kitchen, or would you like to?
  Telephone
  Television
  Stereo or radio
  Home computer
  Other

Safety
Do you need an intercom to link you to your children's rooms, a play yard, or family room?

Do you require a burglar system to lock or unlock your back door or garage?
How safe is your kitchen?
  Electrical outlet placement
  Doorways to the outdoors and to the basement
  Location of cleaning aids or other poisonous substances
  Location of knives and other sharp implements
  Location of fire extinguisher

Collections and Display
What kinds of antiques and collectibles are displayed in your kitchen?

How many of the above do you use, and how many do you simply display?

How are these currently displayed?
  Open shelving
  On the walls
  From ceiling beams
  In cupboards or other major furniture pieces
  On windowsills
  On countertops
  Other
Should you child-proof your collections?

Must you keep collectibles out of reach of the family pet?

Do you collect and display special foods and herbs?

Do you collect cookbooks?

Do you want a separate seating or family-room area in the kitchen?

Do you want a wood stove or fireplace?

The fun and excitement of creating a kitchen begins with ideas, and ideas come from many sources. The primary source is you: Take time to answer the questionnaire; this is the important first step in planning your new kitchen. You may be infatuated with a neighbor's country kitchen that you wish were yours. You may have visited a department store and noticed a display of dinnerware in a fabulous stripped-pine country cupboard and want one just like it in your kitchen—but where? You may have toured a decorators' showhouse and been entranced by ways of applying wall covering and companion fabric and want to reproduce the effect in your kitchen.

One easy way to compile ideas is to save up magazines that zero in on home design. Called "shelter" magazines, these offer ideas for decorating every room in your house. These magazines are often complemented by "special interest" publications which focus on a particular room, such as the kitchen. Gather up as many of these magazines as you can at your local newsstand, supermarket, or library.

If you don't like to cut up your magazines, you might want to photocopy pages of the kitchens and collections you like, for in order to use magazines as real guides and tools, we recommend a hands-on involvement with their ideas. Cut. Clip. Mark. Nothing beats markers, scissors, and tape! Put your clippings temporarily in an accordion file.

Circle products that appeal to you and underline the captions that describe them. Note arrangements of appliances, colors that strike your fancy, and textures too. Whatever interests you on first impression will probably linger in your mind.

Do not ignore the advertising that appears in any of these magazines. Manufacturers place their advertisements here to inform you of their newest products, and you may find that one or more of these innovations will work well in your new kitchen design. Most ads offer a mail-away address so that you can solicit more complete information regarding the product you see in the picture. Often the manufacturers will detail dimensions and finishes, as well as installation information. Usually they also include a listing of dealers in your area who carry their products so that you can arrange to review the product easily in a showroom or retail outlet near you. As you clip, you may want to add more specific facts to your pile of general impressions. The special "booklets" sections in both shelter and special-interest publications invite you to send away for literature that details products currently on the market, all of which should pertain to home design. Take advantage of such mail-in opportunities; also check out the shoppers' sections located at the back of these magazines for other resources that might not be well known.

You will find a wealth of information in the volume from the *Sweet's Catalog* that targets kitchen appliances; this volume looks at literally hundreds of illustrated brochures of products, listed by topic and manufacturer. Your local library should carry this catalog. If you will be working with a professional, such as an architect, designer, or general contractor, who may have the *Sweet's Catalog,* ask if you can peruse it at your convenience.

Do not neglect your *Yellow Pages.* Here you will find listings of local appliance dealers and showrooms that display merchandise you can examine in person. You can gather many ideas from displays—just as a picture is worth more than a thousand words, a look at the "real thing" is worth more than a thousand photos!

A visit to your local lumberyard, hardware store, home-improvement center, or kitchen specialty shop will add more to your stockpile of information. Here, again, you should be able to assemble bunches of brochures, and you can ask questions about installation procedures and costs.

Making an Album
Now that you and your family have answered our

questionnaire and have compiled loads of clippings and notes and brochures, it's time to begin pulling together all the bits and pieces and firming up your ideas.

A good way to begin is with a notebook or album, which will organize and clarify concepts and details. Buy a loose-leaf binder; you can add pages all the time and move pages around, if you want to, later on. Acetate-covered pages, which are thick and easy to work with, offer the most flexibility, for you can simply peel back the acetate, set your information in place, and press the acetate over it. Acetates can be folded back if you want to switch or replace photos.

As mentioned earlier, your questionnaire actually outlined several major areas of concern, and you can tab your album according to these areas. They are:

Layout—the arrangement of appliances and cabinets within the work area

Traffic patterns—the manner in which you move about and through the work area

Appliances—the choices you will make

Storage—space allotments throughout the room

Countertops—surfaces for performing specific tasks

Lighting—general and specific solutions

These major areas will be targeted throughout this chapter. Take notes and transfer your ideas to each tabulated section in your album.

As you go along, take snapshots of every aspect of your kitchen that fits into each problem area and place them in the album. You will find it easier to talk through your ideas if you have a visual document of what actually exists in your kitchen, and you can then supplement this document with the specific illustrations, photos, and brochures of the products you will want instead of what you have now.

You might want to add a photo panorama of the whole room to the page that illustrates your rough plan; you can refer to it as you make doodles on the plan. You get, quite literally, a complete picture this way, and this will facilitate discussions with your architect or contractor later on too.

At the very beginning of your album, set aside a few pages to list your fantasies. Think of everything you ever wanted for your kitchen, no matter what the expense. You may be surprised to find out from your architect that you can, in fact, incorporate some of these particulars into your dream kitchen by making a change or two in another aspect of the design.

Make photocopies of the questionnaire, and place one in the album following the fantasy pages so that you can refer to it over and over. Use other copies to transfer some of your answers to the particular problem areas they cover, but keep a complete set of answers up front so that you will always have documentation of the entire project.

Making a Rough Floor Plan

The most valuable tool for visualizing a new and improved kitchen will be your rough floor plan. A rough floor plan consists of an accurately measured-out sketch of your existing kitchen, drawn out on a sheet of gridded paper. You can buy gridded paper at your stationery or art supply store, by the sheet or in pad form. Buy the kind that is set up in quarter-inch blocks as architects and designers normally calculate one quarter-inch block representing one foot. If you find this scale too small, you may want to draw your floor plan with two or even four blocks representing a foot. If you expand the units, you may have to tape two or more sheets of paper together.

Measurements of the room must be rendered precisely—to a sixteenth of an inch—for the reason that appliances and cabinets must fit precisely in the final plan. As you proceed to measure out your kitchen, use a six-foot folding carpenter's rule, if possible, as yardsticks and retractible tapes tend to slip, resulting in incorrect calculations.

Your first step in setting up a rough floor plan is to draw in a general outline of the room—just a sketch, actually—based on the overall dimensions and config-

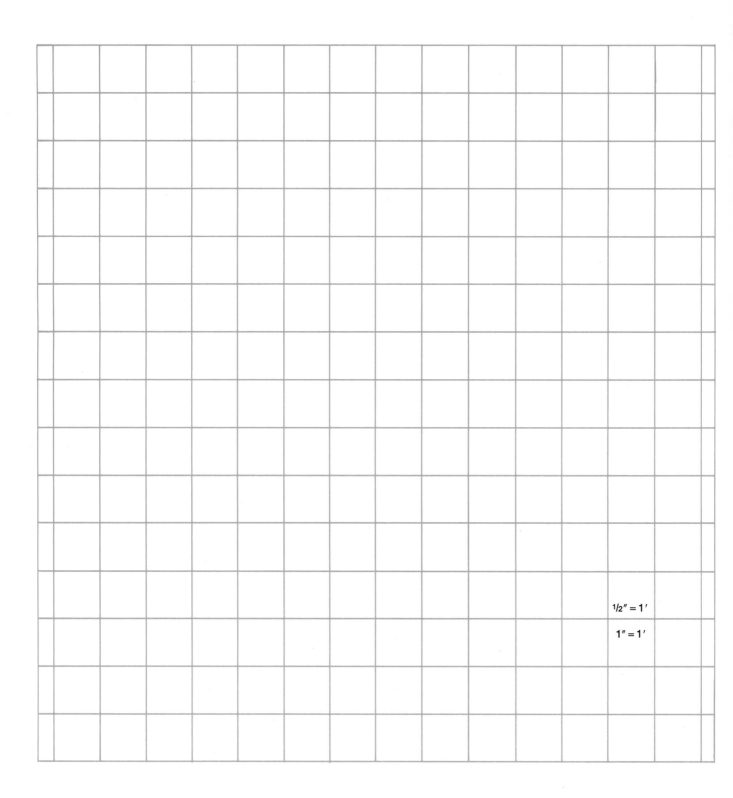

½" = 1'

1" = 1'

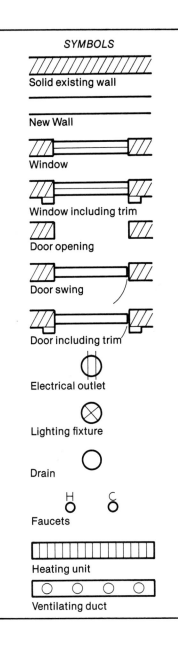

SYMBOLS

Solid existing wall

New Wall

Window

Window including trim

Door opening

Door swing

Door including trim

Electrical outlet

Lighting fixture

Drain

Faucets

Heating unit

Ventilating duct

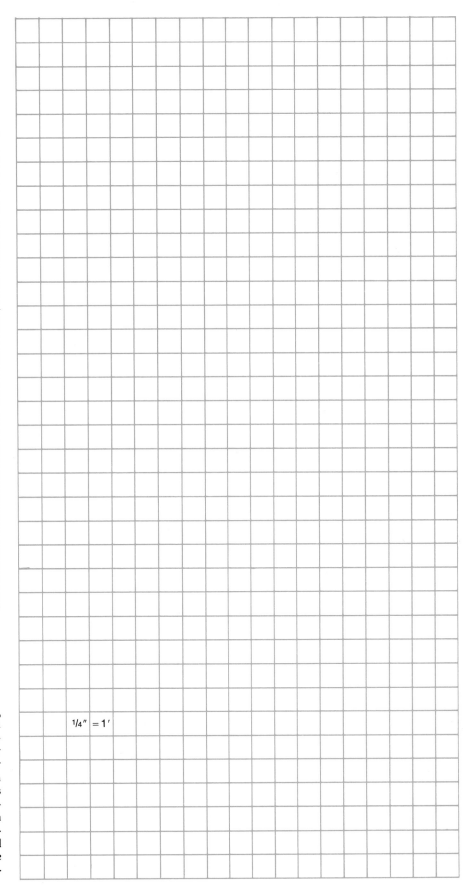

¼" = 1'

Depending upon how big your kitchen will be, work with the quarter-inch-equals-one-foot grid or the half-inch one. The larger grid gives you more room to play with your space plan, but it may take up too much space on your grid page. The smaller grid is one-half the size, and you have to be extremely precise with your markings when you work with a scale this small. The symbols above represent walls and doors and other elements you will have to place on the plan. These are the symbols used by architects and contractors.

189

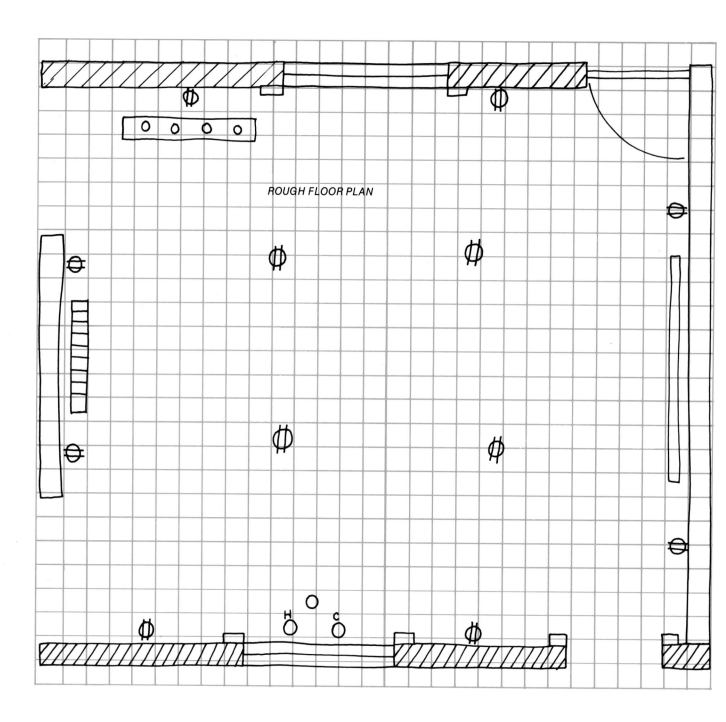

ROUGH FLOOR PLAN

Above: Drawing up the rough floor plan should be a simple exercise; it should not intimidate you in any way. The dimensions must be exact, but the actual sketch can look quite casual. This sketch simply gives you an idea of the "raw" space you have to work with.

Opposite: You can trace these standard appliances—range, refrigerator, dishwasher, sink, and trash compactor—right onto the half-inch-equals-one-foot grid. These represent the most common sizes and shapes, which are usually less expensive too.

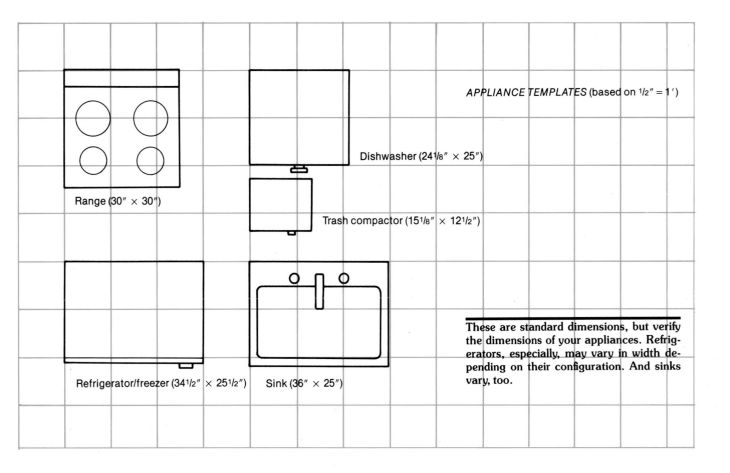

APPLIANCE TEMPLATES (based on ½″ = 1′)

Dishwasher (24⅛″ × 25″)

Range (30″ × 30″)

Trash compactor (15⅛″ × 12½″)

These are standard dimensions, but verify the dimensions of your appliances. Refrigerators, especially, may vary in width depending on their configuration. And sinks vary, too.

Refrigerator/freezer (34½″ × 25½″)   Sink (36″ × 25″)

urations of the space. Then, start at one corner of the room and measure the distance to the first opening or the first obstruction you come across. This may be a door or window or a jog in the wall. If it is a door or a window, measure to the outer edge of the trim; then add the width of the trim itself; then measure across the opening of the window or door; then, across the width of the trim on the other side.

You will now have four separate dimensions on your rough outline. Proceed in this manner all around the edges of the room. Be sure that you indicate every jog or shift as you go. When you are finished, add up the dimensions of each wall; opposite walls should match.

After you gauge your overall measurements, you should write down the heights of the windowsills from the floor, and you should indicate where doors lead and which way they open.

In the margin of your plan, write down the ceiling height, and indicate any soffits over existing cabinets.

You will note that the measurement of the soffit is calculated from the floor to the base of the soffit.

Following the symbols given in the chart on this page, mark on the rough plan where the plumbing line comes into the drain of the sink and to any other existing appliances, such as the dishwasher or washer/dryer. Indicate where electrical outlets currently exist. Make an X with a circle around it on the plan where overhead lighting fixtures are located, and indicate where any heating or cooling elements are set.

Many older houses have walls that lean, and so truly accurate measurements are impossible to calculate. Make sure you know whether or not the corners of the room are precisely squared.

Once everything has been measured, you can sit back and study the rough plan to see what you will want to change. Make several photocopies or tracings of this plan to doodle around on as you try out different ideas. As you proceed through this chapter, do not hesitate to doodle some more!

Now that you have your notebook organized, and have been experimenting with ideas on your rough plan, you must sit down to the task of thinking through just how you want to live and work in your kitchen. A kitchen is composed of several "activity centers." We have indicated these before: They are the areas devoted to preparing and cooking foods, serving meals, eating and/or entertaining, and cleanup. You can add supplementary areas, such as a children's play space, a home office, a menu-planning center, or a wet bar.

On one of your photocopies or tracings of the rough plan, draw circles to indicate where you'd most enjoy locating these various activities. Some activities may overlap, but it is preferable to keep them separate so that you can move from one to the other easily.

As you focus on each of your activity centers, you may find that the best place to begin is with cleanup: the sink. Plumbing lines are difficult and costly to relocate; you can stretch them only a few inches to the right or left of the sink drain.

In many country kitchens, the sink sits right under a window, a preferred location not only for enjoying a view but also for taking advantage of natural light and ventilation. The sink area should be flanked by two sections of counter space: a comfortable 24 inches to the left of the sink and a minimum of 30 inches to the right (if you are right-handed; these measurements should be reversed if you are left-handed). The dishwasher usually tucks in under the counter to the left of the sink, and the trash compactor, if you want one and your building permit allows it, to the right. Again, you may want to reverse these if you are left-handed.

The configuration of the counter space near the sink aids not only in cleanup but also in the preparation of foods that require washing and draining. Such

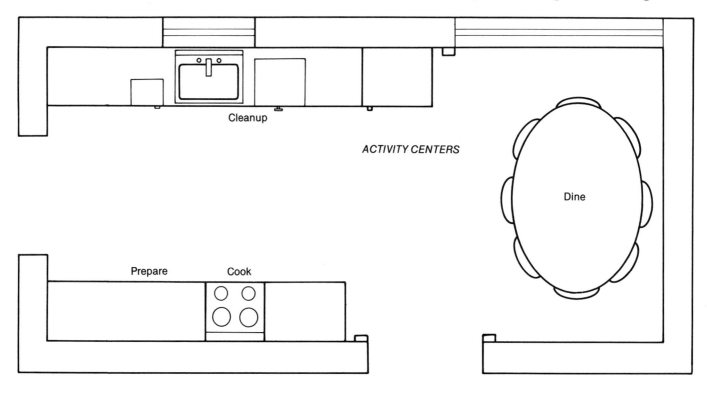

Cleanup

ACTIVITY CENTERS

Dine

Prepare   Cook

countertops become gathering spots, too, for flower arranging and other wet tasks.

The cooking center takes its cue from the range, or from a cooktop/wall oven combination. A microwave oven may figure into this setup too. Again, you may have to take into account an existing gas line, if your range will operate on gas. If you eliminate gas and use only electricity, you can exercise more freedom in your appliance placement. A minimum of 18 inches on either side of the range or cooktop allows for hot-pot layovers before serving; wall ovens require a similar expanse on one side or the other.

The refrigerator requires at least 18 inches of counter space on the side facing the open door—again, for parking foods. For the side-by-side combination refrigerator/freezer, this allotment occurs on the left, opposite the opening of the right-hand refrigerator door.

For preparing foods comfortably, you should count on having at least 36 inches of counter space, which usually stretches between the sink and the range (or cooktop) or between the sink and the refrigerator. The serving counter should extend at least 30 inches and often reaches from the range (or cooktop) toward the eating area.

If you do specialty cooking, such as pastry making, your countertop allotment should include calculations for any separate surfaces, such as marble insets or special chopping blocks. Any countertop used for food preparation must, in addition, be available for small appliances, especially if you want to leave any or all of these out on the counter permanently.

Most counters are 24 inches deep—the depth of most appliances—but you may want to expand yours if you do leave your small appliances out all the time, so that they don't invade your work area. Whenever you adjust the counter, remember to readjust the base cabinets underneath so you do not have too great an overhang.

You will see that you can combine some of these countertop measurements—say, the sink counter in tandem with the food-preparation counter. Once you have tallied up these ideals, you can then juggle your countertop-with-appliances configurations to grant you the best working situation possible.

The Work Triangle

As long ago as 1869, Catharine Beecher and Harriet Beecher Stowe, in their pioneering manual on household activities—*The American Woman's Home*—decried the wasted steps in the preparation of a meal. They recommended closing up the distances between the cooking area, the sink, and the kitchen table. In the 1950s, Cornell University sponsored a series of studies based, in effect, on their revolutionary ideas and came up with the concept of the ideal "work triangle," which reduced steps in the preparation of meals (but not in serving) to a minimum, for comfort and efficiency.

Basically, the work triangle is measured from the center points of the kitchen's three major appliances: from the sink to the range to the refrigerator. The sum of the three sides of the ideal triangle should not exceed 22 feet—too tiring—nor be less than 12 feet—too cramped. In other words, no two appliances should snuggle up closer than four feet to each other, nor should they be set farther apart from each other than nine feet.

You will see, from the following descriptions of basic kitchen layouts, that, except in the narrow one-wall situation, the work triangle can always be worked into any planning scheme.

For the work triangle to be most effective, it should be compact and also self-contained, with no major traffic patterns crossing it. In the corridor configuration this is impossible, of course, as you can see; but in the basic L and the versatile U, such interruptions can be avoided.

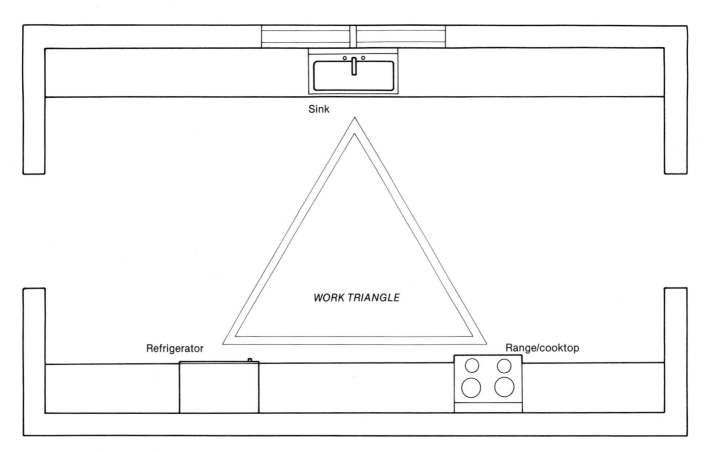

Sink

WORK TRIANGLE

Refrigerator

Range/cooktop

Why the Work Triangle?

Just for fun, let's follow the example set out by Terence Conran in his own *Kitchen Book*. Let's make a quick cup of coffee and see how many steps this takes. First, get your kettle from the cupboard. Take it to the sink and fill it with water. Set it on the range and turn on the burner. Next, pull out your canister of coffee. If you are going to grind your coffee beans, add in the steps for this activity: getting out the grinder and grinding the beans. If you are using instant or freeze-dried coffee, get a spoon out of the cutlery drawer and a mug from the storage cabinet. Measure out the coffee in your mug. Check the kettle to see if the water is boiling, and, if it is, turn off the burner on the range. Pour the water into the mug. (Of course, if you are using freshly ground coffee, you may have extra steps here, entailing specialized coffee equipment such as filters or drip pots.) Are you going to add milk and sugar to your coffee? Where are you going to sit with it? Do you want to turn on the television or radio as you enjoy this cup? Or use the telephone?

Now, check up on how far you traveled to perform this simple task. Can you shift things around to make this process more efficient and less tiring?

Traffic Patterns

The correct work triangle and appropriate arrangement of your appliances will alleviate many wasted steps in your kitchen, but other traffic patterns— how you move through and around the room—must be considered for the comfort of everyone who will gather here.

The work triangle itself functions best when it is not penetrated at all by a traffic corridor such as the passage between the back door and the living areas. Try to circumvent your triangle, and reroute such a passage if possible. The typical "corridor" measures about the same width as a doorway, from 30 to 36 inches. Mark any of these corridors, invisible though they may be, on your rough floor plan. Consider how you travel between the back door and the refrigerator or pantry for unloading groceries; think out how you move from the sink to the serving or cleanup area near the kitchen table; calculate how the children roam from the mudroom to where they play.

When you have planned out the work triangle and any supplementary activity areas, and then marked in the traffic patterns, you may find that you should relocate a door or two. This could increase

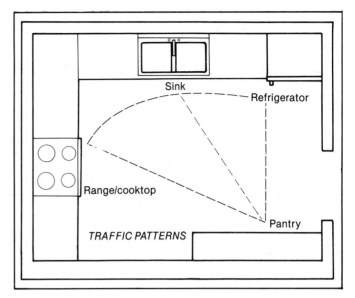

TRAFFIC PATTERNS

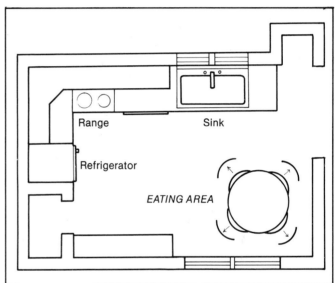

EATING AREA

your budget, of course; ask your architect or contractor for recommendations. It might turn out to be less costly to move your eating area to another part of the room, for example; or it might be cheapest to block up one door altogether and move all traffic in a different direction through the room.

The basic rule of thumb for the amount of space needed for an eating area is to allow at least 12 to 15 square feet per person, which includes placement of the table and chairs plus the space required to move comfortably around this grouping. You can build in a banquette or bench to eliminate some of the space, but then you must anticipate serving from one end of your table or the other, rather than all around. For maximum comfort, plan on at least a three-foot clearance behind each chair, for pulling it out and for moving behind the chair while serving and clearing.

As an aside here: At the table itself, grant each person tabletop space at least 24 inches square, both for the place setting and for elbow room. In other words, a square table should measure a minimum of four feet on a side for a family of four; four by six feet would prove more tolerable. A round table used by a family of four should measure three feet in diameter.

If you build a snack bar or use a peninsula or island for dining, again allow a passageway of at least three feet behind the chairs or barstools; remember, too, that everyone needs at least 20 inches of legroom under the countertop.

Appliances and cabinets located across from each other must be separated by a four-foot-wide aisle so that opposite doors may open simultaneously.

Specialized activities require certain amounts of free space. A home office or menu-planning center, for instance, should measure at least 24 inches in width, with the three-foot clearance behind to pull back a chair; again, allow 20 inches for legroom underneath the desk surface. A wet bar should embrace at least a 4-foot-square work area, so that two or more people can converge in the space and chat at the bar sink and counter while preparing drinks.

STANDARD DIMENSIONS

Corridor:	30–36 inches wide
Eating area:	12–15 square feet per person
Tables and chairs:	36-inch clearance behind each chair
	minimum of 24 inches square per person for table top
Countertops:	36-inch clearance behind each chair or stool
	20-inch legroom under counter
Door swings of appliances:	30–36 inches plus clearance across the corridor

The One-Wall Kitchen

The one-wall kitchen is just that: It extends along one wall, usually right in a living room or living/dining room. Or the one-wall kitchen may be self-contained in a separate, skinny room that has a dead end.

For maximum efficiency this wall should extend a minimum of 15 feet; if the kitchen is self-contained, it will need a minimum of three feet between the appliances and the opposite wall.

The one-wall kitchen efficiently centers on the sink, with the range and the refrigerator at opposite ends. Counters between them should measure 24 inches and 36 inches, respectively. An additional 18 inches at the other side of the range proves useful for hot pots, and also as an insulation barrier between the range and the wall.

If the one-wall kitchen is wider than five feet, but narrower than the eight feet necessary to convert it to a corridor kitchen, you can add a set of narrow cabinets along the opposite wall for extra storage. The lower cabinets can be capped with a narrow countertop to double as a buffet.

The Corridor Kitchen

The corridor kitchen extends along two walls, preferably with a door at either end. As there are no corners to be calculated into the overall design, the corridor kitchen is a model of efficiency. The work triangle can be positioned precisely, utilizing both walls. The major obstacle to the corridor configuration is the traffic pattern; all movement through this space obviously passes right through the work triangle.

The corridor kitchen must reach to at least eight feet in width, to allow appliance and cabinet doors opposite each other to open easily. Because the corridor kitchen is such a good layout, counter space is maximized to greatest advantage. The most efficient arrangement for the corridor is with the sink centered on one wall and the refrigerator and the range opposite with counter space between them, to make the work triangle exact.

If the corridor swells in width to at least 19 feet, an island can be added for further flexibility. If you do add an island, it should measure at least 24 inches across and 78 inches in length, so that an inset range or

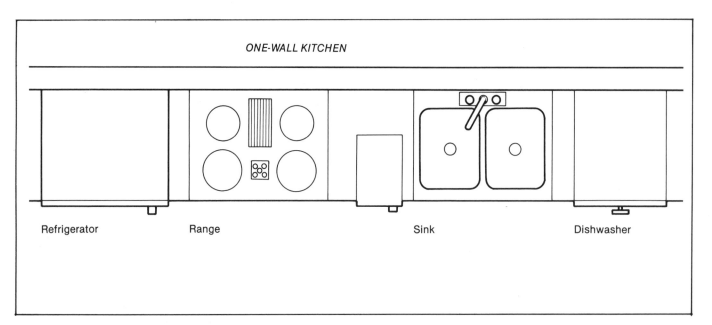

ONE-WALL KITCHEN

Refrigerator   Range   Sink   Dishwasher

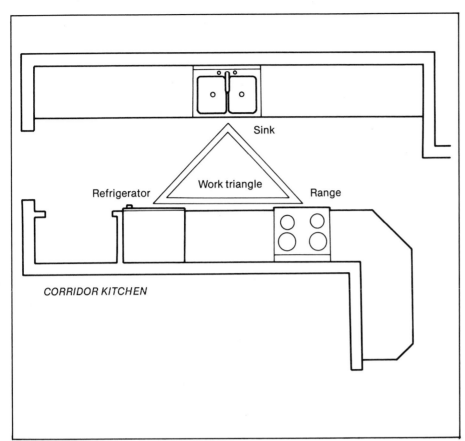

Sink

Refrigerator   Work triangle   Range

CORRIDOR KITCHEN

The floor plans on the following pages show the variations possible in any space, large or small. The working triangle is recommended for efficiency, but in some cases where a room is particularly tiny or narrow, this solution is out of the question. In the case on the opposite page, the one-wall configuration works well.

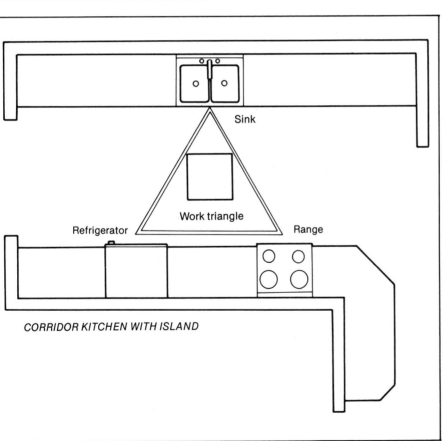

Sink

Refrigerator   Work triangle   Range

CORRIDOR KITCHEN WITH ISLAND

The work triangle can easily absorb a center island, with traffic patterns running right around it. The island thus becomes handy to all three major appliances, and supplements working surfaces. Storage may be provided underneath on all four sides.

cooktop will be embraced by adequate counter space. The major consideration regarding an island is electrical; wiring would have to be extended under the floor to the range. And, too, if you choose a cooktop with specialized downdraft venting, the correct system will have to be installed, again underneath the floor and reaching to an exterior wall. In any case, avoid placing the refrigerator and the range opposite each other. There may be instances when both doors need to open, and this would obstruct your maneuvers in the corridor.

The U-Shaped Kitchen

Of all kitchen designs, the U-shaped layout has proved the most popular, for it adapts readily to all sorts of tasks, and it works as efficiently in a small space as it does in a large room. The work triangle is enhanced in this setup, as distances are equalized by the flexible placement of the major appliances along the base and two "legs" of the U. Often one leg of the U extends beyond the range to incorporate an eating counter; again, as with the peninsula in an L-shaped kitchen, this leg may act as a room divider as well.

When considering the placement of the appli-

ances, you will realize that the sink can be situated conveniently under a window, or it can just as easily slip into the leg of the U that acts as an eating counter—great for cleanup after a meal. Or perhaps you want two sinks, one under the window for food preparation and another for dishwashing only.

In the U-shaped kitchen, the base of the U should extend at least 8 feet, although 10 to 12 feet is preferable to avoid feeling cramped in the interior area defined by the U. The leg that embraces the refrigerator should run at least 48 to 60 inches, and the leg accommodating the range or cooktop should reach at least 66 inches. If the sink and dishwasher are located in one leg, that leg should extend 72 inches. These are minimums, remember, and so try to add extra inches if you can, for more elbow room.

If the U-shaped kitchen is very wide, an island may be inserted somewhere between the two legs, thus affording not only another countertop but also the potential for locating a cooktop or extra sink. If either or both are installed in the island, the island should measure at least 38 inches in width to avoid spatters and splashes.

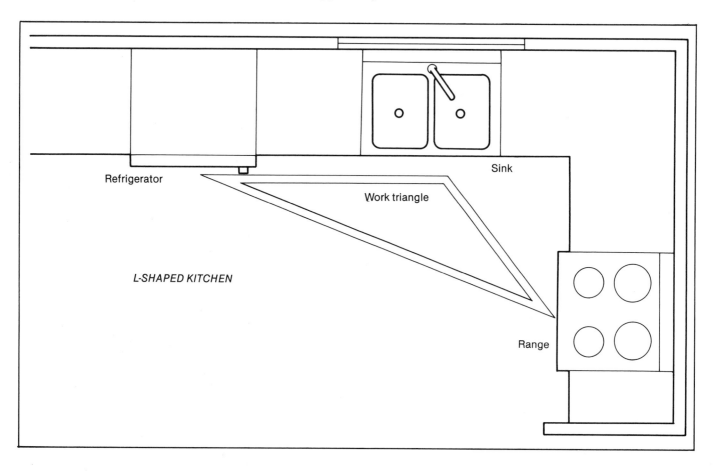

Refrigerator

Sink

Work triangle

L-SHAPED KITCHEN

Range

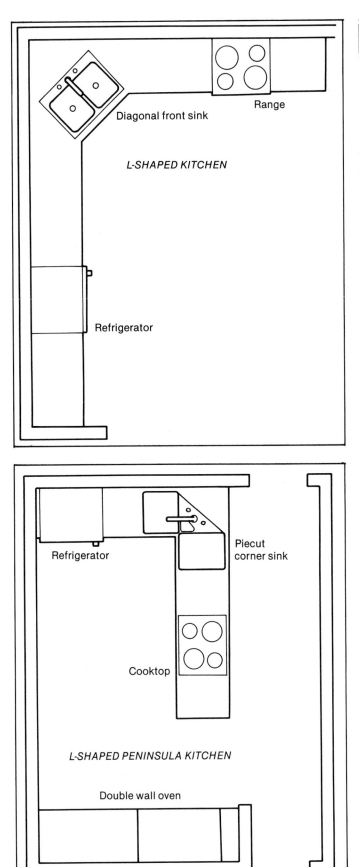

Range

Diagonal front sink

L-SHAPED KITCHEN

Refrigerator

Refrigerator

Piecut
corner sink

Cooktop

L-SHAPED PENINSULA KITCHEN

Double wall oven

The L-Shaped Kitchen

The L-shaped kitchen can be created from the corner made by two adjacent walls, or by extending a peninsula from one wall so that the work triangle is contained within the resulting L. The peninsula, useful as a room divider, also can provide an eating surface if its countertop is cantilevered so that barstools can be pulled up underneath.

The most efficient work triangle for the L comprises the refrigerator at one end of the L, against the wall, with counter space extending from it to the sink and then on to the range and the serving center.

Turning the corner of an L sets up a potential obstacle to using the corner space effectively, but this can be avoided by inserting a corner cabinet in this position outfitted with a lazy susan inside. Or you can place the sink in the corner instead, setting it at an angle or installing it as a double-bowl "pie," which positions one bowl on either side of the actual corner. As some space beneath the sink will be lost, consider placing the garbage pail here.

The countertop space necessary for the efficiency of the L works out as follows: Beginning with the refrigerator against one wall, run a minimum of 24 inches of counter from the refrigerator—to its right, say—to the sink, passing across the top of the dishwasher; to the right of the sink, add 18 to 24 inches, and after the corner is turned, add another 18 to 24 inches leading to the range or cooktop. Another countertop, measuring at least 18 inches, leads off to the right of the range, and, if a cooktop is used instead, the wall ovens complete the end of the L.

When one leg of the L is a peninsula, of course, the wall ovens will have to be located on another wall, preferably opposite the opening of the L.

In the L-shaped kitchen, be sure to keep the appliances away from the corner; crowding in this area inhibits ease of movement and creates obstructions. When appliance doors are opened, they may bump into each other.

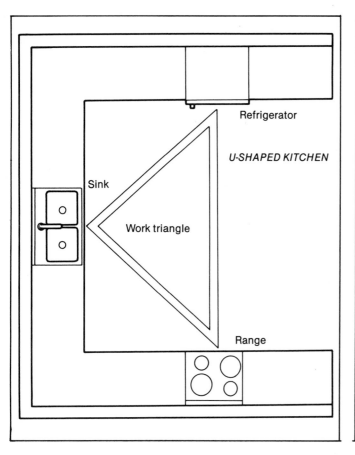

Refrigerator

U-SHAPED KITCHEN

Sink

Work triangle

Range

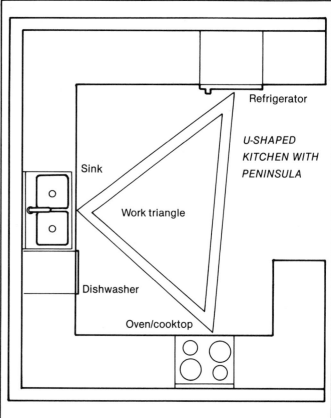

Refrigerator

U-SHAPED KITCHEN WITH PENINSULA

Sink

Work triangle

Dishwasher

Oven/cooktop

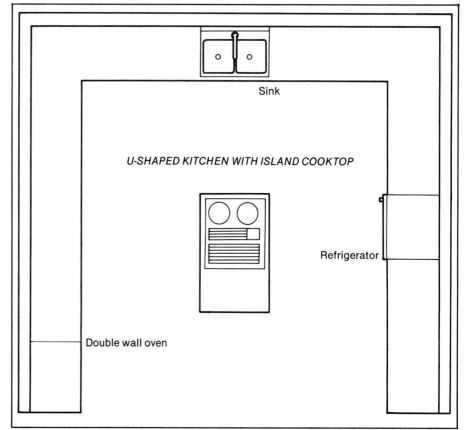

Sink

U-SHAPED KITCHEN WITH ISLAND COOKTOP

Refrigerator

Double wall oven

The L-shaped kitchens on the two preceding pages and the U-shaped kitchens on this page offer many solutions to the design of a generous space. Appliances need not lock into any one position to work well in the triangle; many variations are possible, depending in part on other factors—the arrangement of cabinetry, for example, or the addition of an island or a prized antique such as a cupboard or pie safe.

any of the major appliances available today seemingly perform miracles. Some even talk to you! Electronic controls, computerized readouts, and built-in safety features distinguish many appliances and are marks of household sophistication and convenience. Such features, of course, do not come cheaply; you will have to research just how elaborate and costly you want any single appliance to be.

The alternatives are myriad, and only the basics are reviewed here, to give you a general guide. There are two major considerations: First, how much gadgetry do you really require? And second, and most important of all, will everyone in your family be able to operate the selected appliances without danger or confusion?

If you are concerned about maintaining country style in a convenient, modern kitchen, do not be dismayed by the supposedly "contemporary" look of many major appliances. Black glass, for example, harmonizes beautifully with deep-toned traditional wood cabinetry, and enameled colors such as almond, bone, silver, and pewter marry handsomely with paler woods and laminates. Stainless steel is a good foil, too. If you want a distinctly traditional look, you can select from among many appliance panels that can match wood grains exactly, in any color or tonality. Panels are available to match laminated countertops, and you can even design your own panels if you are working with an architect who can get them made.

APPLIANCE	WATTAGE
Range	12,200
Microwave oven	1450
Roaster	1425
Toaster	1400
Deep-fat fryer	1200
Dishwasher	1200
Fry pan	1200
Griddle	1200
Portable broiler	1140
Refrigerator freezer (14 cu. ft) Frost-free	615
Coffee maker	600
Garbage disposal	445
Freezer (15 cu. ft) Frost-free	440
Trash compactor	400
Freezer (15 cu. ft) Manual defrost	341
Refrigerator freezer (14 cu. ft) Manual defrost	326
Refrigerator (12 cu. ft) Frost-free	321
Manual defrost	241
Window fan	200
Slow cooker	200
Television (color, solid state)	200
Blender	150
Stand mixer	150
Can opener	100
Ice crusher	100
Carving knife	95
Juicer	90
Hand mixer	80
Knife sharpener	40
Radio	25
Clock	2.5

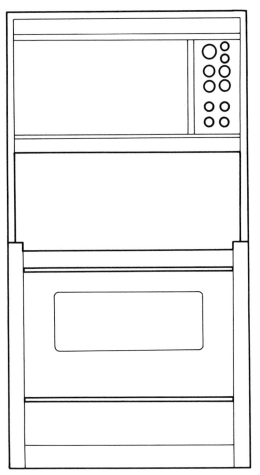

Double-oven range

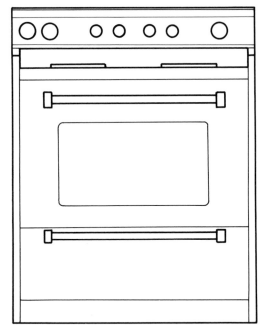

Freestanding range with separate hood

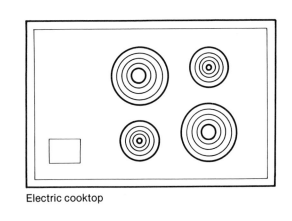

Electric cooktop

Gas cooktop

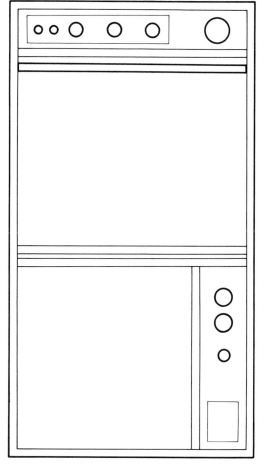

Built-in double wall oven

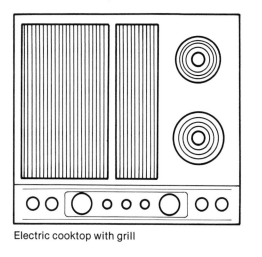

Electric cooktop with grill

When you review the energy-efficiency ratings of your appliance choices, note, too, how much electricity each one actually uses. You may need to install separate wiring for each new appliance, especially if local building codes require it. Normally the stove, dishwasher, refrigerator, and washer/dryer need separate circuits so that no system will overload. Other appliances, such as portable broilers and toasters, eat up a lot of electricity and should run along a circuit that will accommodate them separately from any major appliance nearby.

Additionally, any electronics—such as television, home computer, or intercom/burglar system—might be considered separately. Where will you place these items in your overall scheme? Locate all of them on your rough plan and indicate generally where wiring comes in now; your architect or designer can then plan a wiring setup that will work for the whole room.

Appliances for Cooking

You have a choice when it comes to cooking appliances. You can consolidate all your cooking and work with a range, which may combine two ovens—even one standard oven with a microwave or microwave/convection oven—and burners. Or you can divide up the cooking and work with a cooktop in tandem with a wall oven or pair of wall ovens. Again, the wall ovens may both be the standard type, or one may offer a microwave capability.

All three—range, cooktop, and oven—may operate on gas or electricity. If a gas line already exists in your kitchen, it is a good idea to retain it for a gas range or cooktop; if an electrical failure occurs in your neighborhood, you can still prepare a meal. If you have small children, you also may find gas a safer option, for the flame is always visible when the gas is turned on. Because an electric coil loses its red-hot appearance before cooling, it is dangerous to the unsuspecting child or adult.

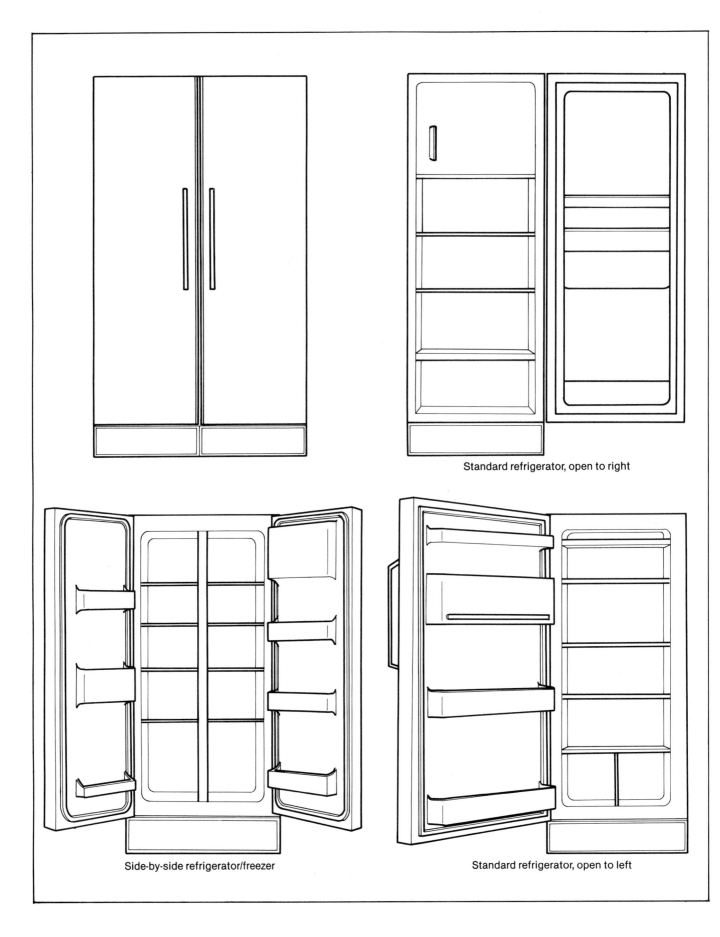

Standard refrigerator, open to right

Side-by-side refrigerator/freezer

Standard refrigerator, open to left

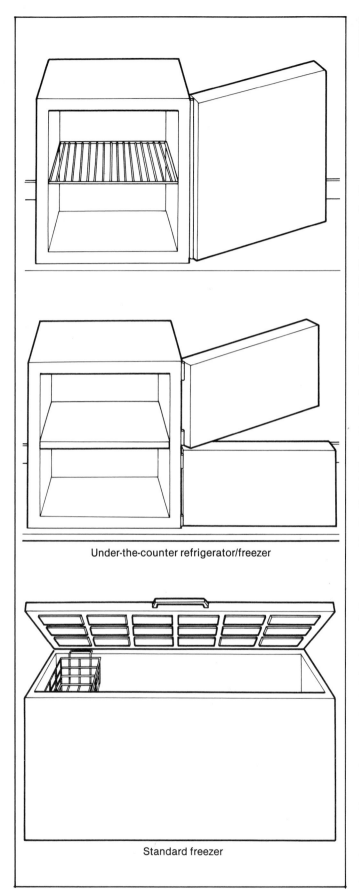

Under-the-counter refrigerator/freezer

Standard freezer

On the other hand, electricity is also convenient, and the simmer-heating is more stable. Electric ovens often provide a more even heat for baking.

Ranges. Ranges come classified as freestanding, slide-in, or drop-in types; most ranges are installed between base cabinets and are insulated to prevent overheating or burning of these adjacent pieces. Ranges are available in a variety of sizes and configurations. Commercial gas ranges, preferred by many active cooks, tend to be extremely bulky, but the multitude of burners—six and sometimes eight—and grill/griddle options offer great flexibility. Residential ranges vary from a narrow 20-inch width suitable for small apartments up to the standard, which is 30 inches, and occasionally even a 36-inch width. The most economical ranges offer a single oven, but overhead ovens have become increasingly popular, especially with the microwave option. Electric ovens often provide a self-cleaning or continuous-cleaning mode, perfect for the maintenance-conscious cook.

Hoods. The grease, smoke, moisture, and odors associated with rangetop cooking should be vented to the outside of the house. Ducted ventilating hoods can attach directly to the wall, soffit, or ceiling, and can vary greatly in size. Wall-hung hoods tend to be compact, from 6 to 30 inches high, a maximum of two feet deep, and from two to four feet long. Ceiling hoods can be double the size, or more, especially if custom-designed.

Ductless hoods filter out grease and smoke, but they do not remove heat, moisture, or odors; these hoods must be cleaned often. When a range incorporates an overhead oven into its design, a ductless hood may be built into the underside of that oven.

Wall ovens. Commonly installed in conjunction with a cooktop, wall ovens are usually powered from the

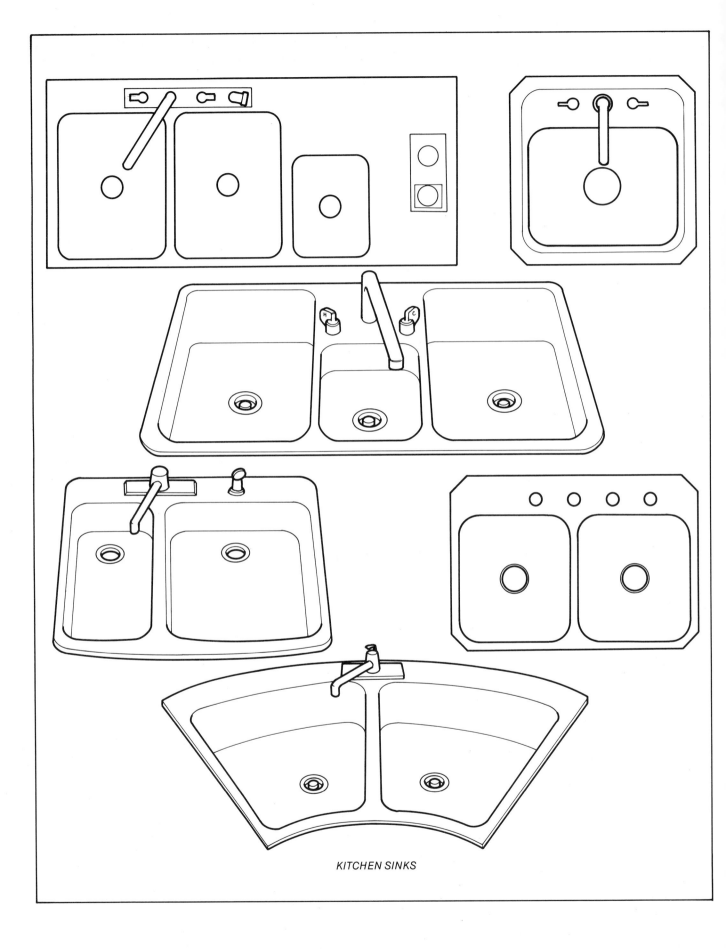

KITCHEN SINKS

Countertop dishwasher

Dishwasher

same source—either gas or electricity. Wall ovens are often paired, for convenience, and newer sets may include a microwave oven set over a standard unit. Electric wall ovens should offer a self-cleaning or continuous-cleaning option, and many wall ovens have removable doors for ease in transferring foods from countertop to oven and back. For the double-oven configuration, allow 50 inches in height, 27 inches in width, and 24 inches in depth before planning the cabinet surround.

A microwave oven—set in the wall, installed over a range, hung under a cabinet, or standing alone—offers the convenience of quick thawing frozen foods and virtually instantaneous reheating of leftovers. Because microwave cooking is so fast, though, it requires constant monitoring, especially for turning foods or browning. Look for timers, temperature probes, and safety turn-off features for foods that don't require as much attention. Microwave cooking also requires special utensils: Metals and enamelware cannot be used; microwave-safe plastics and glass, as well as ceramics and paper, can be. When you purchase a microwave oven, be sure to train every member of your family who will use it in its safe operation.

A convection oven may be installed in tandem with a conventional unit, or it may stand alone. The convection process is somewhat cooler than ordinary cooking, and faster. Convection cooking works best for roasts and baking cookies, but not as well for cooking moist foods such as casseroles or for broiling. Convection ovens remain cool on the outside and need not be vented.

Cooktops. Cooktops drop into a countertop or an island just as a sink would. Power connections—either gas or electricity—are located beneath the unit. Electric cooktops may include a variety of interchangeable modules, such as a grill, griddle, or rotisserie, as well as supplementary burners. Some cooktops, in both power modes, provide downdraft venting, which eliminates the need for an overhead hood. Cooktops range in size from three to six inches high by 29 to 36 inches wide by 19 to 22 inches deep. Many cooktops are crafted from stainless steel, although some are available in an enameled finish in various colors.

Electric smoothtops, made with a treated glass surface, have defined areas that heat up, and they require special smooth-bottomed pots and pans for preparing foods. In addition, they must be cleaned with special aids which will not mar the glass. Smoothtops take a long time to cool down and so they are recommended only for households without children.

Magnetic induction cooktops, which look like ceramic panels set in a steel surface, always remain cool, for the heat transfers from the cooktop to cookware—made of iron and steel only—magnetically.

Commercial gas cooktops stand independently on the counter on short, sturdy legs, but they are not mobile, as they must connect to an existing gas line. Gas cooktops usually have six burners.

Appliances for Storing Foods

The storage of foods is a prime concern, especially for those foods that must be refrigerated or frozen. If you stockpile foods, such as sides of beef or quantities of garden vegetables from your annual harvest, your storage needs multiply. Consider whether or not you will want to have two separate appliances, one just for freezing, and look over your floor plan to determine where to place the additional appliance. Usually, the standard refrigerator-freezer combination bolsters one point on the work triangle, and the additional unit is located in the pantry or in the cellar.

Refrigerators and freezers. Refrigerators, freezers, and combination units are the bulkiest appliances you will buy. Because of the location of the cooling elements on most models, refrigerators and freezers pro-trude beyond the standard 24-inch cabinet depth; only one brand, which places the cooling unit on top, offers a series of 24-inch-deep models.

To gauge your needs, figure on an eight- to ten-cubic-foot capacity for the refrigerator/freezer for each of the first two people, and add one cubic foot per additional person. For a family of four, therefore, a 22-cubic-foot refrigerator should suffice.

As you consider your shopping habits, you can decide whether you will need a separate freezer. You might opt for a freezer that is equivalent in size to a refrigerator, pairing them. Or you might want to use a chest-type freezer and locate it elsewhere, such as in the basement. If you buy sides of meat or put up loads of garden vegetables, you might want to plan for this particular option.

Sizes of the most commonly available refrigerator/ freezer combinations vary widely. The freezer-above version offers the widest range, from 14 to 32 cubic feet. Popular side-by-side combinations, which are more costly, run from 19 to 25 cubic feet. Upright freezers offer from 13 to 21 cubic feet, and chest freezers, from 9 to 18 cubic feet. Consider, too, under-counter models which can supplement your needs, especially in a separate wet-bar area. These provide a bit more then four cubic feet, both in the mini-refrigerator and mini-freezer versions.

It costs less to operate a full refrigerator, and so you need to be exact in your calculations of how much space you will need to stock foods on a daily basis.

Other considerations are: Do you want to include an ice maker in your unit, or a cold-drink dispenser? Would you like the self-defrost option? And, lastly, be sure to specify the direction in which the refrigerator door should open; it should open toward the adjacent countertop.

Appliances for Cleanup

When you evaluate your food preparation and

8-inch or 10-inch chef's knife	Tongs	12-inch size, with lids
6-inch vegetable knife	Can opener (if not electric)	Cast-iron casserole, preferably enameled,
3-inch paring knife	Corkscrew	2- or 3-quart size
8-inch to 10-inch serrated bread knife	Vegetable peeler	Lasagna dish
Carving fork	Grater	Rack (for using lasagna dish as a roaster)
Two or three wooden spoons	Measuring cup	Cake tins
Stainless steel serving spoon	Measuring spoons	Pie dish
Stainless steel slotted spoon	Set of mixing bowls	Food mill
Wire whisk	Strainers, one big and one small	Salad spinner or salad basket
Spatula	Colander	Steamer insert for saucepan
Ladle	Saucepans, one 1-quart, one 1½-quart, and	Storage containers for leftovers
Rolling pin	one 2-quart size, with lids	Oven mitts with asbestos liners
Rubber or plastic food scraper	Frypans, one 6-inch, 8-inch, 10-inch, and	Trivets

cleanup routines, think of how big a sink you will need, or if, in fact, you should make space for two.

Sinks. Sinks most commonly are found with single bowls in a variety of sizes and shapes, but you will also be able to order special, larger-size versions with a double- or triple-bowl. Some sinks have a shallow bowl, with a drain rack inset, for working with foods, and a deep bowl for soaking pots and pans. A triple-bowl sink often has a narrow center bowl, which is handy for soaking cutlery. Some sinks offer a choptop inset too.

Stainless steel is commonly chosen for its durability; the 18-gauge weight, which has a higher chrome content, is stronger than the 20-gauge weight. Other types include enameled cast iron—it is heavy, durable, easy to clean, and comes in colors—and also enamel-on-steel.

Sinks usually arrive predrilled for faucet assembly. You choose or purchase faucets separately, and so you may want to consider single-lever models as opposed to separate hot and cold faucets. Consider, too, additional options, such as a soap dispenser, instant hot- and cold-water dispensers for coffee, tea, and other beverage setups, and a spray attachment on a hose.

You can choose a sink with a self-rim which drops into the countertop; a sink that can be installed flush with the countertop and outlined with a narrow band; or a sink that is recessed into the counter so that the thickness of the counter forms a framing rim.

Dishwashers. Standardized to measure 24 inches square, and 34 inches high, dishwashers usually slip right in under the counter next to the sink. You can choose a portable model if you don't have the space for a built-in; portables are usually capped with a chop-top, and they roll on casters up to the sink, where they hook up to the water supply with special hoses.

Look for energy-saving features, above all; cycles can vary, according to the nature of the wash-up task, from simple rinsing to pot scrubbing. Drying cycles may be heated or not.

The main consideration is the configuration of the racks inside the unit; check to see how glasses will fit, and whether or not there are lift-out sections that will allow you to accommodate large pots and pans.

Garbage disposals. Garbage disposals attach under the drain in your sink and can accommodate certain food wastes in batches. The cap to the disposal twists to turn the unit on. The major consideration here: Check to be sure your building code permits the use of a disposal; some cities do not allow disposals to be installed because of the difficulty of removing waste.

Trash compactors. These slender units compress garbage into a waste bag that weighs about 20 to 25 pounds when filled, thus eliminating many bags full of bulky trash. Trash compactors slide in under the counter wherever they are needed, most commonly near the sink. Most compactors are built-ins, but free-standing units on casters are also available.

To ascertain how much storage space you will need, take a long, close look at your shopping patterns, eating habits, and entertaining style, and make a list of your current inventory of foods, dinnerware, and kitchen utensils. Your list will be a chart to which you can refer as you figure out what should go where. Against this list, calculate just how much room each product or group of products takes up; how many inches, for instance, are occupied by a stack of dinner plates, by a group of mugs, or by all your boxes of breakfast cereal.

At this point, it may occur to you that certain items take up lots of space but are used rarely, if ever. Do you really want to hold on to something you use hardly at all? Can you give it away without missing it later on?

When you set up your storage-planning chart, think of alternative modes of using space. You can solve a problem in a number of ways. For example, rather than stacking teacups on a shelf, you can hang them on cup hooks under a shelf.

It makes the most sense and simplifies matters if you locate each item, or group of items, nearest its activity center. Breakfast dishes should be stored near the breakfast nook or kitchen counter where the children eat each morning; by contrast, if you use different dishes at night for eating in a dining room, you may want to move those dishes out of the kitchen altogether, or place them nearest the dishwasher.

Try not to stack too many different items together; it is easier to keep things separate for better access, and you will be less likely to break or spill or mess up as you work. Consider labeling your storage shelves with what you plan to put on each. This helps children and guests when they want to find a particular dish or food.

The major mistake with any kitchen storage plan is, quite simply, *too much stuff*.

When planning storage in your wall cabinets, work up and down from eye level. For that national average, the woman who is five feet four inches tall, eye level occurs at about four feet eleven inches. Between shoulder and eye level, you should keep your most-used dishes and foods. For safety's sake, store heaviest items in base cabinets near the floor, and the least-used, but lighter, items on the topmost shelves in your wall cabinets.

If you are planning to combine open and closed storage, list what you want to display, as opposed to what you don't mind hiding away.

As a safety precaution, if you have young children in your household, never place cleaning aids or other poisonous substances under the sink or in base cabinets. Keep them out of reach. For this reason, too, it is best to place garbage in a clamp-top pail that children cannot pry open.

Open Storage

Open shelving creates a backdrop for dinnerware, kitchen utensils, and collectibles. Usually ranging along the walls, shelving can run the entire length of a room for dramatic effect, or it can simply be concentrated in one area. A narrow shelf running along under the ceiling can take the place of a soffit and will provide an eye-catching surface for special small collections.

Shelving can be narrow or very thick, depending upon the lumber you choose. Boxy configurations will separate specific groups of items, while continuous shelving leads the eye on and on.

Another form of open storage is the plate rack. Antique racks often exhibit several tiers, each compartmentalized for dishes, bowls, or platters. Plate racks can hang from the ceiling or rest on a countertop. Other types of racks, especially the more commonplace modern plastic-coated wire racks, work well right over the sink, where plates may simultaneously dry and add a spark of display savvy. Folding

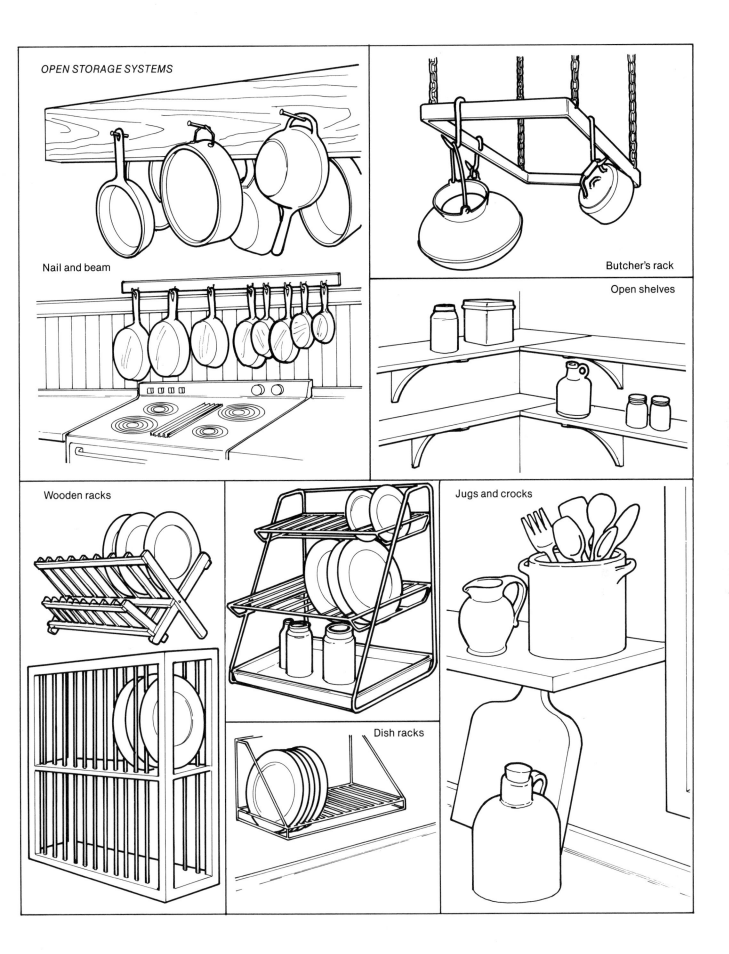

OPEN STORAGE SYSTEMS

Nail and beam

Butcher's rack

Open shelves

Wooden racks

Jugs and crocks

Dish racks

211

wooden racks, usually used alongside the sink, can instead be grouped all along a countertop to hold many items as well as plates and cups.

Butcher-style racks, with thick hooks, can be hung over an island or table to keep frequently used pots and pans at arm's reach, and to show off favorite colors and textures, such as copper or enamel.

Pegboard is a time-honored solution to open storage. Pegboard comes in four-by-eight-foot panels, which your lumberyard can cut down to measure for your wall; you can install pegboard behind doors, too, to gain additional storage space. You must maintain a bit of distance between the board and the wall or door for the insertion of hooks. You can make a frame for the board from furring strips, or you can simply insert plumber's washers every foot or so along the perimeter of the board.

Take an organizational cue from Julia Child if you opt for pegboard: Mrs. Child and her husband, Paul, outlined each pot and pan on the board; the silhouettes then remind them where to put everything back after it has been used.

Plastic-coated wire grid panels, in a variety of sizes, can be installed wherever you need them. Organizers, such as spice shelves and cutlery pockets, hang from the grid, as do various hooks. A grid proves especially useful near the sink or in the laundry for stashing wet gear.

Bins, caddies, and roll-around carts give you supplementary storage options that are mobile and versatile; just remember to save room to park them.

The architectural impact of ceiling beams is dramatized in the country kitchen by the display of hanging pots and pans, baskets, herbs and garlic, and other small collectibles.

Choosing Your Cabinets

Because they are so highly visible and take up so much space, the cabinets you select for your kitchen will quickly establish the style and mood of the room. Cabinet styles range from sleek and clinical to warm and cozy. You will find different kinds of wood looks, as well as many colors of laminate. Some laminates simulate textures, too, such as barn siding.

Cabinets come in several types: knock-down stock cabinets arrive unassembled, and you (or a hired professional) must put them together; factory-built modular stock cabinets are available in a series of standardized sizes that mix and match to produce the look you want; special-order cabinets go beyond mere standardization by offering a greater variety of built-in storage crannies as well as myriad accessory options; and, finally, custom cabinets are handcrafted by a cabinetmaker according to specifications set down by you and your architect or contractor.

Knock-downs are the least expensive, of course. Usually fabricated of particleboard with a wood-look veneer, they are easy to install but will not last as long as ready-built or custom-built cabinets.

Factory-built stock cabinets are the most common solution to storage. The least expensive versions may, again, be constructed of particleboard; a higher price will bring cabinets with a plywood core. Stock cabinets are modular; they range in width from a minimum of nine inches and increase in three- or six-inch increments up to 48 inches. Modular units fit together to form a complete "run," or length, of storage, according to your needs. Wood looks are traditional for this type of cabinetry, but occasionally laminates are also available.

Special-order cabinetry, specified by your architect or designer takes that extra step toward personalizing your storage. Special-order cabinets come in a greater choice of materials and boast finer finishes. You can ask for a specific wood, for instance, such as oak or pecan, and you can request hand-staining rather than a spray-on finish. Some built-ins which prove handy include lazy susans for corner cabinets, pull-out drawers in base cabinets for pots and pans, and notched spice or cutlery drawers. Some special-order cabinet companies even offer drawers in their baseboards. You will have a greater selection of hardware to highlight your cabinets, from simple architect-preferred U-pulls to old-fashioned brass knobs.

At the top of the line are custom-designed and custom-crafted cabinets, built by a cabinetmaker to your exact specifications. The cabinetmaker treats each individual cabinet as a piece of furniture, right down to the dovetailing in the drawers.

Major considerations, for any cabinetry you choose should be: Are the joints sturdy and solid; and are they glued or nailed securely? Do drawers slide in and out with ease? Are doors hung and hinged securely? Do door and drawer fronts feel solid and substantial?

You would be wise to leave three or four inches on either side of a window before you start a wall cabinet series, to allow for shutters, curtains, or any other window treatment; leave the same margin on either side of a door. If you have wide trim surrounding your windows and doors, you can plan to abut cabinetry to the trim for a clean line.

Cabinets hanging over the refrigerator need an inch or two of "breathing" room; some refrigerators provide a grill to connect to the cabinet.

The cabinet over the range must be located at least 30 inches over the cooking surface; some cabinets adapt for the installation of a microwave oven or a venting hood.

Cabinet trim is available to surround wall ovens; you must know the wall oven's exact dimensions before specifying trim measurements.

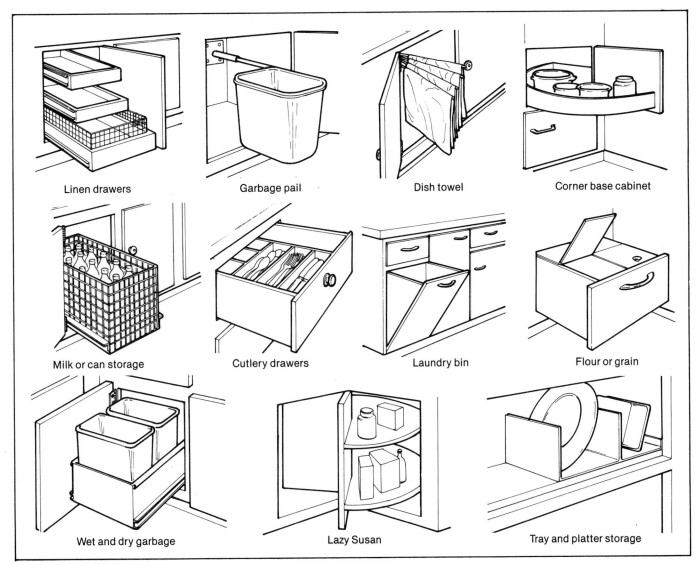

Linen drawers

Garbage pail

Dish towel

Corner base cabinet

Milk or can storage

Cutlery drawers

Laundry bin

Flour or grain

Wet and dry garbage

Lazy Susan

Tray and platter storage

And, remember, above all: Devise the placement of your cabinets so that their doors do not interfere with appliance doors or with your traffic patterns.

Base Cabinets

Base cabinets, including toeplates and countertops, have been sized according to an equation based on the "average" woman of five feet four inches, with a comfort factor of 36 inches as a convenient working height for preparing foods. The base cabinet itself is normally $30^{1}/_{2}$ inches high; the toeplate lifts the cabinet another 4 inches, and the countertop adds a final $1^{1}/_{2}$ inches to the overall dimension.

If you are shorter or taller than this average, you can adjust the height of the base cabinets by altering the height of the toeplate or by adding a narrow drawer between the cabinet and the countertop.

To calculate the right counter height for you: With your elbows at your sides, establish a comfortable position for chopping or measuring, and have a companion measure from your hand to the floor. Will 36 inches indeed be right for you? Many people, even of that average five feet four inches, find that $37^{1}/_{2}$ inches is more comfortable. If you have bought stock cabinets, you can always place a butcher-block chop-top on top of the counter for that extra inch or so.

Base cabinets normally extend 24 inches from the front back to the wall; add an extra inch for the countertop overhang. Most appliances, except for the refrigerator, align with this dimension. If you anticipate garaging a series of small appliances along your countertop, though, you may want to expand it, adding a few inches to its depth so that you maintain a good work surface in front of those appliances. If you are custom-designing your cabinets, they, too, can be extended those extra inches in depth. Note that if you line up small appliances in a row, an electrical outlet strip would be a convenience, for each appliance could plug right into its own socket.

If you do expand your countertop, an extra shelf or rim will run behind the appliances that line up with these cabinets; this can be convenient for storing small items. A small shelf behind the sink, for example, can hold soap, a sponge and liquid detergent, a series of small herbs in pots, or even a few pretty ceramics.

Accordingly, you can standardize your cabinet run and countertop to align with the appliance that juts out the most—the refrigerator—and this will give you more room for food preparation as well as those little added shelf areas discussed above.

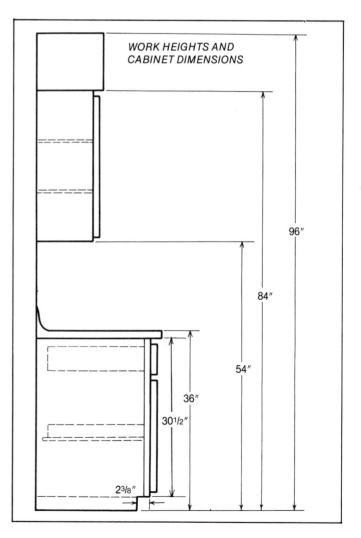

WORK HEIGHTS AND CABINET DIMENSIONS

96"

84"

54"

36"

$30^{1}/_{2}$"

$2^{3}/_{8}$"

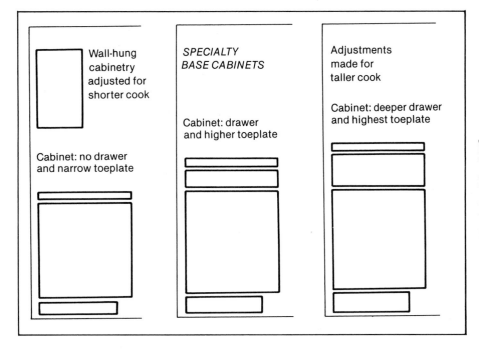

Wall-hung cabinetry adjusted for shorter cook

Cabinet: no drawer and narrow toeplate

SPECIALTY BASE CABINETS

Cabinet: drawer and higher toeplate

Adjustments made for taller cook

Cabinet: deeper drawer and highest toeplate

Everyone has a different and individual "comfort" zone, or level for working, according to his or her height. Most cabinetry has been standardized, based upon a norm of five feet four inches. Perhaps you will want to raise or lower your work surface to suit your style. You can do this easily by building up the base under the cabinet, adding a drawer atop the cabinet, or thickening the work surface itself. A butcher block, for example, can be purchased in different thicknesses. Similarly, overhead cabinets can be adjusted for easy accessibility, and need not conform to standard height.

Note, too: If you decide to raise your cabinets to a more convenient height, you will have to raise the adjoining appliances—especially a range—so that the tops remain flush with the countertops.

Special Cabinets

When cabinets turn a corner, a dead space results. To rectify this situation, special corner cabinets are available which provide accessible storage within. The most convenient have lazy susans inside, which revolve to hold pots and pans or foods. Lazy susans, or carousels, come in 33-, 36-, or 39-inch sizes; the 36-inch option is the most popular version used in conjunction with standard cabinetry.

Corner cabinets may be specified in tandem with a corner sink unit; the sink may be a single bowl set at an angle or a double bowl in a "pie" configuration.

You may also want to specify special tall cabinets, which will align with the top of your wall cabinets, to provide room for a pantry or a broom closet.

Wall Cabinets

Wall cabinets expand in width as base cabinets do, and line up with them for a clean, organized look. When wall cabinets are stacked over their matching base cabinets, allow a 24-inch margin between the countertop and bottom of the wall cabinets for working ease.

Again, based on the average five-foot-four-inch woman's height, it has been calculated that a person this size can most easily reach up to a height of 68 to 71 inches; wall cabinets commonly extend to 84 inches and then a soffit, or faked wall strip, runs from the top of the cabinet to the ceiling. You can leave that area open, however, and utilize the top surface of the run of wall cabinets to display pots and pans or kitchen collectibles, such as baskets, firkins, butter tubs, and the like.

If you custom-design your cabinets, you might want them to reach all the way to the ceiling so that you can use the topmost areas inside for storing rarely used items, such as holiday platters. If you cannot reach many of your upper shelves, keep a stowaway or footstool on hand; you can store this under the sink or in the pantry.

Wall cabinets are usually 12 inches deep, which is satisfactory for the storage of most foods and for most dinnerware.

Smaller wall cabinets work into the overall scheme for placement over the refrigerator or over the range. When these are installed over the range, plan to attach a hood to the cabinet. Some foreign-made wall cabinets have been designed especially for placement over the sink; these subdivide inside for dinnerware storage, and they have no bottom so that just-washed plates and dishes can drip and dry right into the sink.

The various surfaces in your kitchen—walls, floors, countertops, and ceilings—reflect the most personal choices of all building materials in your design scheme. The kitchen, however, is the room most prone to dirt build-up, from grease to spills, so consider the maintenance of all surfaces above all else.

Walls

Of the four surfaces, walls signal first; there are more of them! Options abound, from paneling to brick to paper to paint, or a mix of two or more.

Of the above, a paint job costs the least, offers myriad visual effects in terms of color and texture, and is easy and quick to apply. In fact, if you can't afford an entire remodeling, you can get a quick lift and makeover just with a coat of paint.

Because the kitchen builds up grease and soil from cooking, even with proper ventilation, you should consider a paint surface with a sheen, which wipes down easily. Paints come in a variety of looks: Flat paint will absorb stains and spots and is difficult to maintain in the kitchen; an eggshell finish offers a slight luster. Semigloss and high-gloss finishes swab efficiently.

Paint colors number in the hundreds. Check swatch booklets, and take home sample cards to try out. Check these in daylight and in artificial light—both incandescent and fluorescent—and by candlelight too. Colors change their appearance, depending upon the light. Many homeowners opt for convenient and inexpensive white as a backdrop that appears crisp and clean; white comes in both cool and warm tones.

Bright paints such as yellow and orange perk up a space, but use them with caution: Such colors set up a high-intensity, high-glare situation which is hard on the eyes over the long haul, especially when you are concentrating on recipes and the steps involved in food preparation. Consider, instead, using a more muted shade to tone down reflections and highlights. Deep jewel tones provide a dramatic background for foods and collectibles; many of the "colonial" colors fall into this category, although some colors may be grayed slightly, again to be easier on the eyes. Deeper colors tend to shield and mask dirt longer.

Wall coverings for the kitchen can be found in specialized collections geared specifically to this room, or they may be unearthed in collections that present more general styles you might be happy with, such as mini-prints, provençal prints, stripes, or checks. Patterns that mirror kitchen motifs, such as herbs and spices and flowers, are perennial favorites. The most important factor to consider is, as with paint, scrubbability. Many wall coverings are sold with the claim that they can be wiped clean in a flash, but check to be sure the paper is vinylized or treated to be moisture-resistant. You can stall soil buildup on standard papers by spraying them with plastic coating spray.

Many vinyl wall coverings are prepasted so that you can install them yourself. Your dealer will help you calculate how much you will need, based upon the single roll, even though most papers arrive in double or even triple rolls. Widths commonly average between 20 and 28 inches, and you will find five yards (or about 30 square feet) on the average roll. To calculate: Measure the perimeter of your room and multiply it by the height of the ceiling; then subtract the wall areas that would not be covered (doors, windows, cabinets, appliances). Divide by 30, which is the length of one roll. Note, however, that every pattern has a "repeat"—the length it takes for a pattern motif to reappear—and you should add this amount to your total to compensate for lining up the pattern correctly across the room from roll to roll. Your dealer can figure this out for you, for the repeat will be tagged on the paper of your choice. Don't forget, too, to add in a few inches at the top and the bottom of each strip to be hung, almost as if you were allowing for the hem of a dress. This will give you leeway for any error.

If you install your wall covering yourself, remember that it will not adhere to a dirty or greasy surface, and so you must clean the walls meticulously before application. Cracks must be filled and bumps smoothed.

Wall paneling conceals many an imperfection, including bumpy or uneven surfaces, and paneling lasts a long time. Paneling comes in a variety of modes: solid wood, veneered plywood, and veneer over fiberboard that has been protected with vinyl. Wood-grain looks, both light- and dark-toned, as well as weaves, textures, and stripes, plus brick, stone, and stucco looks, all prove popular. Paneling works best on accent walls, to show off collections and accessories. It is not recommended for areas around the range, ovens, or sink, for it does not resist heat or moisture well; conversely, however, paneling is handy for service areas where a quick dusting can keep it clean.

Ceramic tile, like paneling, works best for accent walls, such as backsplashes behind the range and sink. Ceramic tile shrugs off moisture well and is impervious to heat. With many colors and patterns to choose from, tile becomes a perfect visual accessory. Be sure to ask for wall tile, though, for tiles are fired for different purposes, and what will work on the wall will not stand up to traffic on the floor. Wall tiles come in many sizes, from tiny hexagons to mosaics to squares that measure up to a foot on each side. Grouting now can complement tile colors, as it is available in several hues, not simply a basic cream tone.

When you calculate your tile needs, build in another ten percent or so for breakage, and for splitting or splicing in hard-to-reach areas. Edging tiles for walls are called bullnose tiles; figure in the linear dimension of the surface you want to finish off to ascertain how many of these you will need. Add in corner tiles as well. Or have your dealer make these calculations.

Tiles are not easy to install; it is best to hire a professional or have your architect or dealer suggest one. If you do decide to install your own tiles, remember to start at the center of the surface you will cover and work outward in all directions. This establishes a visual anchor; because of this, though, you will certainly have to cut and fit at edges and corners for a harmonious look. Consider quick-setting adhesives and study their method of application, for this will speed up the installation process significantly. And, note: Follow the manufacturer's directions explicitly because it is extremely difficult to remove tiles once they are set.

Floors

Because you stand and walk so much in the kitchen, flooring is of vital importance, and you should take time to make a decision here based on comfort as well as on design.

For the country kitchen, many people find wood a popular choice. Oak stripping, for example, set tongue-in-groove, looks warm and lasts a long time, especially when it is treated with polyurethane to repel moisture and spills. Pine planks are softer and require more care, as they pockmark easily, but pine looks honey-rich and is a time-honored selection. Woods require professional installation, especially if laid in any sort of pattern, such as a herringbone or parquet. Wood parquet tiles for the do-it-yourselfer are available, however, and they are simple to lay.

Ceramic tiles specified for floors are increasing in popularity, especially the big, bold terra cotta versions from Mexico. Other colors and textures are available, highly glazed or with a matte finish, and you can set up a counterpoint of colors on the floor for a dazzling visual effect. Tiles, as mentioned earlier, are best installed by a pro. Remember, too, that tiles are extremely hard, and they can be slippery and noisy too. So-called quarry tiles, those terra cotta types, can be bought unglazed, but if they are not treated with a special sealer, they have a tendency to absorb grease and stains.

The softest flooring you can choose is made of vinyl and may, in addition, boast a cushioned backing. When purchased in sheet form, vinyl flooring usually measures 6 or 12 or 15 feet across, and you then calculate the length you will need to fit your room. Vinyl flooring proves exceedingly durable and easy to maintain, especially with a no-wax finish. Professional installation, again, is recommended here, but, if you are very handy, you can set vinyl flooring in place yourself. Check to see if a special adhesive is required, and be sure you have the correct cutting tools for snipping around the bases of your appliances and cabinets.

Easier to work with are vinyl tiles, which measure 8 or 12 inches square. These may offer the same no-wax finish as sheet flooring, and you can select from among a great range of patterns and textural effects. The least durable tiles, made of asbestos, chip with rough wear, but they are inexpensive.

Two alternatives not recommended here are indoor-outdoor or other carpeting, and rubber matting. Carpeting may camouflage dirt, but it attracts and absorbs it and cannot be easily cleaned; rubber is slippery, and the types with raised "buttons" catch foods and dirt particles, which subsequently prove difficult to dislodge.

Countertops

The configurations and dimensions typical to counters in conjunction with base cabinets have been discussed earlier in this chapter. As with flooring, durability and ease of maintenance are key to choosing your countertop material. Have your counters installed by a professional, too; there is much cutting and fitting involved, especially around sinks and any special inserts, plus the splicing of backsplashes.

Many country kitchens call for butcher-block or wooden countertops, which give a warm and cozy cast to the room. Woods also mix handsomely with other surface materials, such as marble or tile. To repel moisture and to inhibit staining, woods may be sealed with polyurethane, or they may be treated with olive or vegetable oil. Sealed woods do tend to scratch and burn. Untreated woods make perfect choptops; butcher block is usually chosen, in fact, to cap a roll-around cart or dishwasher just for this purpose.

Plastic laminate leads the field in variety of designs. Laminates come in many colors, and in textures and patterns that simulate "naturals" such as butcher block, wood grain, stone, marble, and slate. Check for thickness as a clue to quality. One manufacturer offers colors which penetrate the entire thickness of the laminate for a seamless look. Laminates are very easy to clean and are waterproof. A totally uniform look can be given to the kitchen if laminate not only sheathes the countertops but also cloaks the cabinets—inside and out—as well.

Very expensive, but increasingly popular, are marble and granite. Both are hard, durable, and cool, and these materials are often chosen by pastry cooks. A marble inset is a possibility if you like to bake but want a less expensive countertop material overall.

Ceramic tiles, mainly the one- to six-inch squares, set up a lively interplay of color and texture on a countertop but, like marble, are hard to the touch. Tiles should be set very closely together to minimize grouting, and the grouting must be sealed to prevent mildew and soil buildup.

Ceilings

You will have inherited a ceiling that you may simply want to leave alone. The most common solution to the country kitchen look is to strip away the old ceiling to—hopefully—reveal a set of beams with lathing or plasterboard between. Beams are the quintessential ingredient in the country kitchen, it seems, not only for their homey appeal, but also because they allow the avid collector another vantage point from which to exhibit favorite finds.

If you do not want to live with a beamed ceiling, you can simply paint or plaster over your existing ceiling, or you can install acoustical tiles over the entire surface to help block out noise and still grant a textured "rustic" look.

Wall coverings may continue on up and over the ceiling, but they should, as recommended earlier, be vinylized to withstand grease and moisture.

Wood strips running across a ceiling warm up a room considerably and are a cheerful alternative to beams or simple plaster. Polyurethane enhances stripping and counteracts moisture and grease buildup.

Lighting in the kitchen emanates from two major sources—windows and lighting fixtures. The combination of both natural and artificial light enhances any work activity, but each kind of light source must be evaluated separately, as some days can turn out to be dark and dismal, and at night, of course, no outside ambient light remains.

The design and placement of your windows adds an element to the architectural design of the room. Be they multi-paned sash windows, sliding horizontal panes, greenhouse inserts, or bay windows, the type of windows you choose should harmonize with the setting as a whole. Take into account the energy-efficiency factor, though, for in winter glass acts as an escape hatch for heat from the house. Choose double-

or triple-glazed windows to counteract heat loss, and, if you can, specify glare-free glass as well, for it is easier on your eyes, especially on very bright days.

Additional light can be harnessed through skylights or clerestory windows, which are those set above eye level. You might be able to add these types without altering your building scheme or diminishing the homey quality of your decor.

Windows should sit from four to six inches above any work surface to prevent spatters and splashes onto the panes. The ambient light in most kitchens comes from an overhead fixture hung from the center of the ceiling. Think about your various activity areas, and plan your overhead light accordingly. You may want to install a track system to target several areas from a single source. You may adore an old tin chandelier and decide to keep it for atmosphere, supplementing its

Lighting for the kitchen should combine an overall or general source with task-related or pinpointed fixtures. A chandelier, for example, provides a cozy glow for the room, but it would have to be supplemented by under-cabinet lighting to illuminate work surfaces. You may like to have more than one overhead source, highlighting a dining area and also a food-preparation area or a wash-up area.

COUNTRY-STYLE CHANDELIERS

warm glow with rows of under-cabinet lighting tubes to light up all the work surfaces separately. Under-cabinet lighting is an easy solution. The main factor here is choosing the correct bulb for your task. Fluorescent lights are cost-effective and use little energy, but they can drain all foods of the richness of color and texture associated with the joy of preparing a meal. Now, however, many new types of fluorescents are available which more closely approximate daylight. Look for one of these daylight bulbs.

Alternatives to track and chandelier abound. You can drop big glass globe lamps or pendants over an island or over the dining table, to focus on those areas. Or you can recess can-type lights into your ceiling and dramatize areas with circumscribed circles of light. Here, again, count on supplementing these sources with under-cabinet lights.

In general, an overall light, falling on about 50 square feet of a room, should radiate at 175 to 200 watts, if incandescent, and from 60 to 80 watts, if fluorescent. Each work counter should be lit by two 75-watt incandescent lights or a pair of 40-watt fluorescents.

Decorative lighting can add immeasurably to the feeling of your kitchen, even if the fixtures you choose are not specifically oriented toward work areas. Sconces, for example, provide an attractive gleam, as do candles of every size and description.

ssuming that you will choose to work with a professional on any significant renovation of your kitchen, or on full-scale construction of a brand-new room, the earlier you consult the pro, the better. You can tailor your concepts with him or her, and be guided in your explorations of the alternatives with the benefit of professional expertise.

Your choices vary in terms of selecting a pro, and these may be dictated partially by your own savvy: How much can you either do or supervise yourself? How handy are you at basic skills, such as carpentry or painting, for example? And, obviously, what is your budget?

The foremost concern regarding professional expertise is the person's knowledge and judgment of building permits and codes pertaining to your community. Your professional can counsel you on how to comply with codes and can oversee inspection of the various phases of the job—plumbing and electrical work, for instance—so that the final inspection of the job will go smoothly. Your pro will know about zoning variances and other wrinkles too: Can you, for example, add on, or would an addition wander too close to your property line?

Professionals fall into four categories: architects, interior designers, designers affiliated with kitchen dealers, and general contractors. Again, depending upon your own expertise and self-confidence, you can work with the pro of your choice in a number of ways. First, of course, you can hire someone to oversee the entire job, from a preliminary consultation straight through to the unveiling of the finished room. Or you may need only advice and blueprints from an architect and decide to proceed the rest of the way with a general contractor. The main thing is to feel comfortable with your decision. Here are your alternatives:

The architect, by training, not only knows and appreciates the design aspects of planning a space but is also knowledgeable about engineering and all the nitty-gritty of what goes on behind the walls—from electrical wiring to heating/cooling plants to plumbing installations. The architect will make recommendations based on the look you want but will also have an intimate insight into the practicalities integral to a well-designed room. The initial consultation sets the stage for the job. Here you discuss what you have written down in your notebook and go over product brochures; you can make specific requests, and you also can converse about vaguely defined needs. The architect, with your go-ahead, will draw up plans for your approval and will make recommendations regarding appliances, surface materials, and other aspects of the design. If you approve of everything so far, and the architect's recommendations fall within your budget, you can proceed to the blueprint stage, and then, in addition, you can retain the architect to supervise the actual construction. If you do so, the architect will hire the general contractor and subcontractors (those who install specific pieces of equipment and perform special skills, such as plastering) and will visit the site to be sure everything is moving along on schedule and within the budget.

An interior designer works in much the same manner as an architect, but his or her training may not encompass the engineering aspects of the job. In this case, an interior designer often retains an architect or engineer to plan out the practical aspects of the room and to draw up the blueprints for the contractor. The designer can supervise the job and work with the general contractor.

A designer affiliated with a kitchen dealer is usually cognizant of all the variables involved in designing a kitchen, or he or she would not maintain that affiliation. If you like your kitchen dealers and respond to their recommendations for appliances and cabinetry, then you may want to use their designer as well. The contractors retained by the designer will be used to working through the kitchen dealers and will have a good working relationship with the firm. The kitchen dealers and their designer may not have as broad a feeling for design in general, but if you have confidence in your personal style and want to act as your own "finishing" designer regarding wall covering, fabric, and paint, then go ahead with this pro.

The general contractor performs the task of getting the kitchen built according to plans, specifications, and blueprints. If an architect or designer oversees the job, the contractor will consult with this person all along the way. If, however, you yourself take the blueprints to the contractor, from whatever source, then you will be responsible for supervising the job, and you must make sure that no corners are cut and no mistakes made that will not only jeopardize the final look, but also alter the budget. The general contractor supervises the subcontractors in any case, but, again, you should be on the lookout to make sure every task is completed according to the specifications for that task.

Your budget, of course, will determine the scale of the construction or remodeling and may dictate which professional you choose. One rule of thumb in coming up with a total budget is to evaluate the resale value of your house and scale your kitchen in proportion with that overall value. A new kitchen adds to the value, but it should not be so excessive that you would not recoup your investment when you move. If, of course, you do not plan to move, the sky's the limit!

The second rule is to divide your total investment proportionally, as follows: 20 percent for appliances; 50 percent for cabinets (usually a dozen or so of these) and all surfaces; and 30 percent for labor. The equation may vary if you decide to buy extremely expensive appliances, for instance, and simply stock cabinets. Or the labor costs may shoot up if you decide on a great deal of custom carpentry.

A budget is not carved in stone, and you should be aware that prices can increase during the time it takes to get the kitchen built. But most additional costs come about when you change your mind about something. It is mandatory that you go over every single detail of your final plan with the architect and the general contractor, and get every estimate of every task set down in a contract, in writing. Changes, even minor ones, may wreak havoc with a budget and timetable.

When you choose your professional, then, be emphatically certain about the entire picture: what you want and what you can spend. If you are going to take out a home-improvement loan, or a personal loan, let him or her know. (Other loan options, by the way, include borrowing against your life insurance, refinancing your mortgage, and borrowing from a credit union.)

Where to find your pro? If you know the work of a particular architect or designer, ask to see other jobs he or she has done in your locality, especially kitchens. Ask to see the person's portfolio of projects and get names of some clients. Interview other clients and find out whether the professional remained within budget and within the time frame set up for completing the job. Credentials count, too. Many architects are associated with the American Institute of Architects (AIA); many designers, with the American Society of Interior Designers (ASID); and many kitchen planners, with the American Institute of Kitchen Dealers, which has a specialist category called Certified Kitchen Designers (CKD).

Once you have narrowed your selection of people you are considering for the job, get bids from the remaining candidates. Estimates of specific jobs should be spelled out and then an overall bid submitted to you for your perusal. You must have an idea of what every phase of the construction will cost, as well as a breakdown of materials and appliance prices. You do not want to be surprised later on.

If bids vary widely, check on differences and discrepancies. Would corners be cut if you go with a low bid? What is being built into the higher bid? A high bid might reflect a greater efficiency, in fact, if that professional plans on dovetailing certain procedures so that construction would actually take less time.

If you want to do some work yourself, you should still get estimates on those aspects of the job, in case you change your mind about what you end up working on. If you want to purchase materials yourself, get estimates on these too, in case you do not end up buying them yourself. In other words: Think through every contingency.

After going over the bids, you can make your final choice. Remember, though, that the bottom line is not only money: You must have a good working relationship with your pro. If he or she will do a good job for you, making no mistakes or extra changes, and will let you know what is happening all along the way, honestly and directly, then your kitchen will reflect that attitude and turn out to be a satisfying room for you and for your entire family. And, in fact, you may even save money in the long run.

he Directory of Sources includes hundreds of items suitable for today's country kitchen and dining room. Products are organized into twenty-eight categories—from major appliances to woodenware—indicating the wide variety of products available.

Directory
of Sources

Waterford Stanley Cookstove

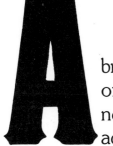

brief listing of the products offered is presented beneath the name and the address of each company, and alongside each company a letter in parentheses designates the following:

(M) -manufacturer; contact for local distributor

(R) -retail; contact directly

(T) -trade; contact through a decorator

(W)-wholesale; contact for a local distribution point

Every effort has been made to ensure the accuracy of the information contained here. With time, however, names and addresses do change, so despite all efforts, this compilation may not be absolutely precise.

MAJOR APPLIANCES

Admiral Home Appliances (M)
1701 East Woodfield Road
Schaumberg, IL 60196
Major appliances

Amana Refrigeration, Inc. (M)
Amana, IA 52204
Refrigerators, freezers, microwave ovens, electric ranges, cooktops

American Crown Gas Stoves (M)
Gray & Dudley Co.
2300 Clifton Road
Nashville, TN 37209
Gas ranges, wall ovens, dishwashers

Caloric Corp. (M)
403 North Main Street
Topton, PA 19562
Major appliances

Chambers Division (M)
Hobart Corporation
Troy, OH 45373
Built-in gas and electric cooktops and ovens

Frigidaire Co. (M)
WC Box 4900
Dayton, OH 45449
Major appliances

General Electric Co. (M)
Appliance Park
Louisville, KY 40225
Major electric appliances

Hardwick Stove Co. (M)
240 Edwards Street
Cleveland, TN 37311
Gas and electric ranges

House of Webster Inc. (M)
Box 488
Rogers, AK 72756
Early American-style wall ovens, electric ranges

Jenn-Air Company (M)
3035 Shadeland
Indianapolis, IN 46226
Electric cooktops, grill ranges, microwave and wall ovens

KitchenAid (M)
Hobart Corporation
Troy, OH 45374
Dishwashers, trash compactors

Sub-Zero (Photo: Bill Hedrich, Hedrich-Blessing)

Magic Chef (M)
740 King Edward
    Avenue
Cleveland, TN 37311
Gas and electric
appliances

Maytag Co. (M)
403 West 4th St. North
Newton, IA 50208
Washers, dryers,
dishwashers, gas and
electric ranges

Modern Maid (M)
403 North Main Street
Topton, PA 19562
Major appliances

Roper Products (M)
1905 West Court Street
Kankakee, IL 60901
Major appliances

Sharp Electronics (M)
10 Sharp Plaza
Paramus, NJ 07652
Microwave ovens

Solinger & Associates (M)
PO Box 196
Clarendon Hills, IL
60514
Garland professional
ranges

Stanley Iron Works (M)
64 Taylor Street
Nashua, NH 03060
Antique cookstoves

**Sub-Zero Freezer
Co., Inc.** (M)
PO Box 4130
Madison, WI 53711
Built-in refrigerators,
freezers

**Tappan Appliances
Division** (M)
Tappan Park
Mansfield, OH 44901
Major kitchen
appliances

**Thermador/Waste
King Products** (M)
5159 District Boulevard
Los Angeles, CA 90040
Major appliances

**White-Westinghouse
Appliance Co.** (M)
930 Fort Duquesne
    Boulevard
Pittsburgh, PA 15222
Major appliances

**Whirlpool
Corporation** (M)
Administrative Center
Benton Harbor, MI
49022
Major appliances

Wolf Range Co. (M)
19600 South Alameda
    Street
Compton, CA 90224
Commercial cooking
equipment

BASKETS

Barton's Baskets (R)
PO Box 67
Forkland, AL 36740
Handwoven split-oak
baskets, custom work
available, mail-order
catalog

Basketry Studio A (R)
PO Box 300
West Barnstable, MA
02668
Traditional and original
basket-weaving kits,
supplies, mail-order

Basketville (R)
Route 1
Putney, VT 05346
Handwoven New
England ash, oak, and
native pine baskets,
mail-order

Coker Creek Crafts (M)
PO Box 95
Coker Creek, TN
37314
White oak baskets,
linens, rugs, catalog

Mrs. J. H. Durham (R)
Route 2, Box 34
Cherokee, AL 35616
Naturally dyed white-
oak splint baskets, mail-
order

Import Specialists (W)
82 Wall Street
New York, NY 10005
Baskets, hemp rugs,
linens, rag place mats

Nancy Scribner, Indian Hill Collection

Indian Hill Collection (M)
N. A. Scribner
PO Box 3767
346 Main Avenue
Norwalk, CT 06851
Natural and dyed
handcrafted reed
baskets, catalog

R. H. Lyons Co., Inc. (W)
270 Denton Avenue
New Hyde Park, NY
11040
Baskets

Primitive Artisan, Inc. (M)
225 Fifth Avenue
New York, NY 10010
Haitian peanut baskets

The Silo (R)
Upland Road
New Milford, CT 06776
Baskets, one-of-a-kind
crafts, furniture, catalog

**Skalmy Basket Co.,
Inc.** (M)
PO Box 846
Shelton, CT 06484
Baskets

Survival Acre (M)
Box 37
Indian Lake, NY 12842
Custom-order willow
baskets
**Vintage Basket
Imports** (W)
PO Box 2105
Yountville, CA 94599
Baskets
**West Rindge Baskets,
Inc.** (M)
93 West Main Street
Rindge, NH 03461
New England-style
baskets, mail-order

BUILDING MATERIALS
Broad-Axe Beam (M)
RD 2, Box 417
West Brattleboro, VT
05301
Hand-hewn white pine
beams
**Carlisle Restoration
Lumber** (M)
Route 123
Stoddard, NH 03464
Wide pine and oak
flooring, paneling, mail-
order
Diamond K. Co., Inc. (M)
130 Buckland Road
South Windsor, CT
06074
Wide pine flooring, barn
wood, beams

Quaker Maid

**Driwood Moulding
Co.** (M)
PO Box 1729
Florence, SC 29503
Period millwork,
embossed and plain
moldings, catalog
Focal Point, Inc. (M)
2005 Marietta Road NW
Atlanta, GA 30318
Architectural moldings
**Hoboken Wood
Flooring Corp.** (M,R)
100 Willow Street
East Rutherford, NJ
07073
Hardwood flooring and
planking, custom
designs
**The House
Carpenters** (M)
Box 217
Shutesbury, MA 01072
Traditional red-oak and
white-pine timber
frame, 18th-century
flooring, molding,
paneling, doors and
doorways, windows

Lord & Burnham (M)
Box 255
Irvington, NY 10533
Greenhouses,
solariums, window
greenhouses
**Louisiana Pacific
Corp.** (M)
111 SW Fifth Avenue
Portland, OR 97204
Waferwood panels
Masonite Corp. (M)
29 North Wacker Drive
Chicago, IL 60606
Building materials, pine-
wood paneling
**Memphis Hardwood
Flooring Co.** (M)
PO Box 7253
Memphis, TN 38107
Plank, strip, and
parquet oak flooring
E. A. Nord Co. (M)
PO Box 1187
Everett, WA 98206
Hemlock and fir
louvered, bifold, and
six-panel doors

W. F. Norman (M)
PO Box 323
Nevada, MO 64772
Authentic tin ceilings,
roof shingles, siding,
catalog
**The Old Fashioned
Milk Paint Co.** (M)
Box 222
Groton, MA 01450
Wide pine flooring and
cabinet boards, old-
fashioned milk paints
**Old World Moulding &
Finishing Co., Inc.** (M)
115 Allen Boulevard
Farmingdale, NY 11735
Custom architectural
paneling, woodwork,
mantels, wall units
Period Pine, Inc. (M)
#6 North Rhodes
  Center N.W.
Atlanta, GA 30309
Old virgin long-leaf
yellow pine, flooring,
paneling, millwork
**Restorations
Unlimited** (M)
PO Box 186
24 West Main
Elizabethville, PA 17023
Restoration consultation
and period millwork
**Vintage
Wood Works** (M,R)
513 South Adams Street
Fredericksburg, TX 78624
Moldings and building
materials

NuTone Housing Group

Wood Moulding & Millwork Producers Association (M)
PO Box 25278
Portland, OR 97225
Trade association represents unfinished-wood-molding manufacturers; booklets on use, installation, and "how-to" of wood products available

CABINETS

Allmilmo Corp. (M)
70 Clinton Road
Fairfield, NJ 07006
European-style cabinets
Ms. Corinne Burke (M)
1 Forest Glenn Road
New Paltz, NY 12561
Custom cabinets, Shaker peg racks, dish racks, accessories, catalog
Coppes Napanee Kitchen Cabinets (M)
Nappanee, IN 46550
Cabinets

Excel Cabinets (M)
One Excel Plaza
Lakewood, NJ 08701
Cabinets
Forms + Surfaces (M)
Box 5215
Santa Barbara, CA 93108
Country wood cabinet pulls and carved wood cabinetry panels
Heritage Custom Kitchens (M)
215 Diller Avenue
New Holland, PA 17557
Cabinets
Merillat Industries, Inc. (M)
PO Box 1946
Adrian, MI 49221
Cabinets
Poggenpohl Corp., USA (M)
6 Pearl Court
Allendale, NJ 07401
Wood and laminate cabinets

Quaker Maid (M)
Route 61
Leesport, PA 19533
Cabinets
St. Charles Manufacturing Co. (M)
1611 East Main Street
St. Charles, IL 60174
Laminate, wood, and steel cabinets
Wood-Mode Cabinetry (M)
Snyder County
Creamer, PA 17833
Wood and laminate cabinets
Yorktowne Inc. (M)
PO Box 231
Red Lion, PA 17356
Wood and laminate cabinets

CEILING FANS

Casablanca Fan Co. (M)
450 North Baldwin Park Boulevard
City of Industry, CA 91746
Ceiling fans, kitchen fixtures, catalog
NuTone, Division of Scoville, Inc. (M)
Madison and Red Bank Roads
Cincinnati, OH 45227
Ceiling fans

Robbins and Myers, Inc., Hunter Division (M)
PO Box 14775
2500 Frisco Avenue
Memphis, TN 38114
Ceiling fans

COOKWARE

All-Clad Metalcrafters, Inc. (M)
RD 2
Canonsburg, PA 15317
Stainless-steel, aluminum, and copper-stainless cookware
Anchor Hocking Corp. (M)
Fifth and Pierce Avenues
Lancaster, OH 43130
Cookware, stemware, dinnerware
Arabia, for Sigma the Tastesetter (M)
225 Fifth Avenue
New York, NY 10010
Finnish enamel cookware, stoneware, glassware, woodenware
Artis Dinnerware (M)
4 Wilton Avenue
PO Box 62
Norwalk, CT 06852
Cookware, dinnerware
Bennington Potters North (M)
PO Box 199
324 County Street
Bennington, VT 05201
Cookware, stoneware, accessories, catalog

CCC International, Inc.

Boston Warehouse (M)
39 Rumford Avenue
Waltham, MA 02154
Cookware, pottery,
stoneware, bowls

Boch Dinnerware (M)
PO Box 675
Perrysburg, OH 43551
Belgian imported
cookware and
dinnerware

Bourgeat Cookware USA, Inc. (M)
281 Albany Street
Cambridge, MA 02139
Copper and aluminum
cookware

Brookville Pottery (R)
Box 848
Brookville Hollow Road
Stockton, NJ 08559
Stoneware cookware and
dinnerware, sponge ware

Club Aluminum (M)
1100 Redmond Road
Jacksonville, AK 72076
Cookware

Commercial Aluminum Cookware Co. (M)
Ampoint Industrial Park
Third and D Streets
Perrysburg, OH 43551
Irish copper cookware,
Calphalon cookware

Copco (M)
2240 West 75th Street
Woodridge, IL 60517
Enamel cookware,
mail-order

Corning Glass Works (M)
Houghton Park
Corning, NY 14830
Cookware, dinnerware

Crate & Barrel (R)
190 Northfield Road
Northfield, IL 60093
Cookware, pottery,
catalog

Dansk Designs Ltd. (M)
Radio Circle Road
Mount Kisco, NY
10549
Enamel cookware,
dinnerware, stainless-
steel flatware

Delaware Pottery (M)
PO Box 105
Hope, NJ 07844
Handmade blue-and-
white traditonal
cookware, stoneware

Denby Tableware, Inc. (M)
130 Campus Plaza
Edison, NJ 08837
Stoneware cookware,
dinnerware, glassware

Pepper Fewel (M)
5803 Galloway Drive
Yakima, WA 98908
Whimsical hand-thrown
and sculptured cookware,
pottery, mail-order

The Foltz Pottery (M)
RD 1, Box 131
Reinholds, PA 17569
Cookware, pottery,
catalog

The French Collection (W)
PO Box 770156
Houston, TX 77215
Imported copper cook-
ware, porcelain, flatware

Gear, Inc. (M)
19 West 34th Street
New York, NY 10001
Cookware, fabric, wall
coverings, linens,
dinnerware, furniture

General Housewares Corp. (M)
PO Box 4066
Terre Haute, IN 47804
White and sponge-ware
enamel steel cookware,
cast-iron cookware

Jacques Jugeat/Philip Stogel Co. (M)
489 Fifth Avenue
New York, NY 10017
French faience porcelain
cookware and
dinnerware

Kosta Boda (M)
225 Fifth Avenue
New York, NY 10010
Porcelain cookware and
dinnerware

Livingston Pottery (R)
Box 74
Livingston, NY 12541
Earthenware and por-
celain cookware, pot-
tery, mail-order catalog

Pfaltzgraff (M)
PO Box 1069
York, PA 17405
Stoneware cookware
and dinnerware

Rauschert Culinary Editions (M)
4 Wilton Avenue
PO Box 62
Norwalk, CT 06852
Oven stoneware,
decorative dinnerware

Directory of Sources

Commercial Aluminum Cookware Company

Regalware (M)
1675 Reigle Drive
Kewaskum, WI 53040
Porcelain-clad and cast
aluminum cookware

**Revere Copper &
Brass, Inc.** (M)
PO Box 250
Clinton, IL 61727
Stainless-steel and
copper cookware

RECO International (M)
138-50 Haven Boulevard
Port Washington, NY
11050
Romertopf terra-cotta
clay cookware, accessories

**Royal Copenhagen
Porcelain/Georg
Jensen Silversmiths** (M)
683 Madison Avenue
New York, NY 10021
Scandinavian-design
copper cookware,
porcelain dinnerware,
lead crystal, sterling
flatware

Royal Doulton (M)
Cottontail Lane
Somerset, NJ 08873
Cookware, bone china,
porcelain, earthenware
dinnerware

**Royal Worcester
Spode Inc.** (M)
26 Kennedy Boulevard
East Brunswick, NJ 08816
Cookware, dinnerware,
earthenware, fine bone
china

Schiller & Asmus (W)
PO Box 575
Yamassee, SC 29945
Le Creuset enameled
cookware, ovenware

Soovia Janis (M)
225 Fifth Avenue
New York, NY 10010
Glazed redware
cookware, dinnerware

**St. Gobain
Glassware** (M)
41 Madison Avenue
New York, NY 10010
French tempered
cookware and glassware

Taylor & Ng (R)
PO Box 8888
2700 Maxwell Way
Fairfield, CA 94533
Cookware, kitchenware

**Trans Duck
International** (M)
2636 Prindle Road
Belmont, CA 94002
Stove-top glass
cookware

Wedgwood, Inc. (M)
41 Madison Avenue
New York, NY 10010
Adams English
cookware and
earthenware

John Wright Co. (M)
Box 40
Wrightsville, PA 17368
Cast-iron bakeware,
catalog

COUNTERTOPS

**Corian Marketing
Communications
Dept.** (M)
Wilmington, DE 19898
Corian products

Formica Corporation (M)
One Cyanamid Plaza
Wayne, NJ 07470
Laminate countertops

Hall Place Tile Shop (R)
2231 Broadway
New York, NY 10024
Countertops, country-
style hand-painted
ceramic tiles, wall
coverings, tile flooring

**Ralph Wilson
Plastics Co.** (M)
600 General Bruce Drive
Temple, TX 76501
Laminate countertops

CURTAINS

Laura Ashley, Inc. (R)
714 Madison Avenue
New York, NY 10021
Curtains, fabrics, linens,
dinnerware, tiles, wall
coverings, mail-order
catalog

**Burlington House
Draperies** (M)
1345 Avenue of the
Americas
New York, NY 10105
Curtains

**Colonial Maid
Curtains, Inc.** (M,R)
Depot Plaza
Mamaroneck, NY
10543
Colonial curtains, mail-
order catalog

Constance Carol (M)
PO Box 899
Building 21, Cordage
Park
Plymouth, MA 02360
Tab curtains, custom
styles, fabrics, stenciled
patterns

Country Curtains (R)
Department 4734
Stockbridge, MA 01262
Curtains, catalog

Curtain Corner (R)
At Paradise Green
Stratford, CT 06497
Curtains, catalog

Great Coverups (R)
Box 1368
West Hartford, CT
06107
Curtains, mail-order

Kirsch Products (M)
PO Box 0370
309 North Prospect
    Avenue
Sturgis, MI 49091
Drapery hardware,
blinds, shades

Old Colony Curtains (R)
Box 759
Westfield, NJ 07090
Curtains, catalog

Rue de France (M,R)
77 Thames Street
Newport, RI 02840
French lace curtains,
catalog

CUTLERY

**W. R. Case & Sons
Co.** (M)
20 Russell Boulevard
Bradford, PA 16701
Cutlery

Fiskars (M)
10261 Yellow Circle
    Drive
Minnetonka, MN 55343
Cutlery and kitchen
utensils

**Gerber Legendary
Blades** (M)
14200 SW 72nd
    Avenue
Portland, OR 97224
Stainless-steel cutlery

**Russell Harrington
Cutlery, Inc.** (M)
44 Green River Street
Southbridge, MA 01550
Cutlery, cooking
utensils

**J. A. Henckels
Zwillingswerk, Inc.** (M)
9 Skyline Drive
Hawthorne, NY 10532
Cutlery, kitchen utensils

Imperial Knives (M)
1776 Broadway
New York, NY 10019
Cutlery

Charles Lapen (R)
Route 9, PO Box 529
West Brookfield, MA
01585
Hand-forged cutlery,
custom wrought-iron
hardware and
chandeliers, mail-order

DECORATIVE
ACCESSORIES

**The American Country
Store** (R)
969 Lexington Avenue
New York, NY 10021
Decorative accessories,
antique and
contemporary china,
flatware, table linens,
mail-order

The Yankee Peddler/Burkart Brothers, Inc.

**American Folk Art,
Ltd.** (R)
PO Box 5211
Hilton Head, SC 29938
Folk-art accessories,
handcrafted baskets,
pot racks, vine wreaths,
catalog

Ms. Corinne Burke (M)
1 Forest Glenn Road
New Paltz, NY 12561
Custom cabinets,
Shaker peg racks, dish
racks, accessories,
catalog

Cardinal China Co. (M)
Cardinal Building
High Street, Box D
Carteret, NJ 07008
Gourmet accessories,
white china dinnerware,
storage jars, earth-tone
crocks, mail-order

Constance Carol (M)
PO Box 899
Building 21, Cordage
    Park
Plymouth, MA 02360
Tab curtains, custom
styles, fabrics, stenciled
patterns

**Colonial Candle of
Cape Cod** (M)
Hyannis, MA 02601
Candles, kitchen
accessories

**Colonial Williamsburg
Foundation** (M,R)
PO Box CH
Williamsburg, VA
23185
Decorative accessories,
documented furniture,
hardware, dinnerware
from Williamsburg
Collection, catalog,
mail-order brochure

**Deerfield
Woodworking** (M)
PO Box 275
Deerfield, MA 01342
Curtain rods, paper-
towel racks, trivets,
mail-order

Elizabeth Eakins (R)
1053 Lexington
    Avenue
New York, NY 10021
Tiles, trays, plates,
trivets; custom-made
handwoven, braided,
and hooked rugs

General Time (M)
520 Guthridge Court
Norcross, GA 30092
Clocks
Heiligenthal Imports (W)
PO Box 5022
Austin, TX 78763
Schleisen ceramics,
Swiss copper molds,
German wax molds
**Hitchcock Furniture
Co.** (M)
New Hartford, CT
06057
Handcrafted and
traditional decorative
accessories and
furniture
Homestead Supply (W)
PO Box 15444D
Pine Hills, FL 32808
Trivets, mail-order
**Howard Kaplan's
French
Country Store** (R)
35 East 10th Street
New York, NY 10003
French antique and
reproduction decorative
accessories, furniture,
dinnerware
**Meiselman Imports
Division** (W)
Rubel & Co.
225 Fifth Avenue
New York, NY 10010
Portuguese and Italian
ceramic accessories

Pfaltzgraff

**The Museum of
American Folk Art** (R)
125 West 55th Street
New York, NY 10019
Handcrafted decorative
accessories for the
kitchen
**D. A. Rinedollar,
Blacksmith** (M)
PO Box 14
Augusta, MO 63332
Wrought-iron corn
dryers, taper dryers
The Silo (R)
Upland Road
New Milford, CT 06776
One-of-a-kind crafts,
baskets, furniture,
catalog
Daniel Strawser (M,R)
126 Main Street
Stouchsburg
Womelsdorf, PA 19567
Hand-painted folk-art
wood carvings, mailorder
The Village Stenciler (M)
25 South Mill Street
Hopkinton, MA 01748
300 Early American
wall and floorcloth
stencils, catalog

**The Westfield Country
Collection** (R)
427 South Avenue W
Westfield, NJ 07090
Decorative kitchen
accessories, catalog
The Yankee Peddler (R)
Burkart Brothers Inc.
Verplanck, NY 10596
Colonial reproduction
tinware accessories,
lanterns, saltboxes,
candlesticks, mail-order
catalog

DINNERWARE
**The American Country
Store** (R)
969 Lexington Avenue
New York, NY 10021
Antique and
contemporary
dinnerware, decorative
accessories, flatware,
table linens, mail-order
**Anchor Hocking
Corp.** (M)
Fifth and Pierce Avenues
Lancaster, OH 43130
Dinnerware, stemware,
cookware

Artis Dinnerware (M)
4 Wilton Avenue
PO Box 62
Norwalk, CT 06852
Dinnerware, ovenware
Laura Ashley China (M)
41 Madison Avenue
New York, NY 10010
Laura Ashley patterned
dinnerware
**Bing & Grondahl
Copenhagen
Porcelain, Inc.** (M)
111 North Lawn
     Avenue
Elmsford, NY 10523
Danish porcelain and
stoneware dinnerware
Block China (M)
11 East 26th Street
New York, NY 10010
Dinnerware, china
products
Boch Dinnerware (M)
PO Box 675
Perrysburg, OH 43551
Belgian imported
dinnerware and
ovenware

Gear Inc.

Breininger Pottery (M)
476 South Church
　　Street
Robesonia, PA 19551
Earthenware
dinnerware, catalog

Brookville Pottery (R)
Box 848
Brookville Hollow Road
Stockton, NJ 08559
Stoneware dinnerware
and cookware, sponge
ware

Cardinal China Co. (M)
Cardinal Building
High Street, Box D
Carteret, NJ 07008
White china
dinnerware, gourmet
accessories, storage
jars, earth-tone crocks,
mail-order

**Colonial Williamsburg
Foundation**
PO Box CH
Williamsburg, VA 23185
Dinnerware from
Williamsburg
Collection, decorator
accessories,
documented furniture,
hardware, catalog, mail-
order brochure

Corning Glass Works (M)
Houghton Park
Corning, NY 14830
Dinnerware, cookware

Crisa (M)
1201 Richardson Drive
Richardson, TX 75080
Glass dinnerware and
stemware, old-
fashioned jars and
pitchers

Dansk Designs Ltd. (M)
Radio Circle Road
Mount Kisco, NY
10549
Enamel dinnerware,
cookware, stainless-
steel flatware

**Denby Tableware,
Inc.** (M)
130 Campus Plaza
Edison, NJ 08837
Stoneware dinnerware,
cookware, glassware

Deruta of Italy (M)
225 Fifth Avenue
New York, NY 10010
Handmade and painted
Italian majolica
dinnerware,
earthenware

Fitz and Floyd (M)
PO Box 815367
Dallas, TX 75381
Country-design
porcelain and
earthenware
dinnerware, accessories

Gear, Inc. (M)
19 West 34th Street
Dinnerware, cookware,
fabric, wall coverings,
linens, furniture

**Ginkgo International,
Ltd.** (W)
5107 Chase Street
Downers Grove, IL
60515
Imported stainless-steel
and melamine
dinnerware, flatware

Marion Grebow (R)
c/o The Gazebo
660 Madison Avenue
New York, NY 10021
Hand-painted porcelain
dinnerware, custom
colors available

Hartstone, Inc. (M)
PO Box 2626
Zanesville, OH 43701
Dinnerware, stoneware,
clay bakeware

Haviland Limoges (M)
11 East 26th Street
New York, NY 10010
French provincial
porcelain dinnerware

**Hutschenreuther &
Arzberg** (M)
41 Madison Avenue
New York, NY 10010
Dinnerware
Mail-order address:
Country Classics
PO Box 586
North Branford, CT
06471

**Iron Mountain
Stoneware** (M)
Laurel Bloomery, TN
37680
Stoneware dinner- and
ovenware, hand-
painted tiles

**Jacques Jugeat/Philip
Stogel Co.** (M)
489 Fifth Avenue
New York, NY 10017
French faience
porcelain dinnerware
and ovenware

Kemp & Beatley, Inc.

Jori Hand Cast Pewter
(M,R)
Bucks County
Pewterers, Inc.
1776 Easton Road
Doylestown, PA 18901
Hand-cast pewter
dinnerware and flatware

**Howard Kaplan's French
Country Store** (R)
35 East 10th Street
New York, NY 10003
French antique and
reproduction
dinnerware, decorative
accessories, furniture

Kosta Boda (M)
225 Fifth Avenue
New York, NY 10010
Porcelain dinnerware
and ovenware

**Ralph Lauren Home
Furnishings** (M)
1185 Avenue of the
    Americas
New York, NY 10019
Dinnerware, fabrics,
linens, flatware,
furniture

Lenox (M)
Old Princeton Pike
Lawrenceville, NJ
08648
Dinnerware, candles,
china

Seymour Mann (W)
225 Fifth Avenue
New York, NY 10010
Porcelain and ironstone
dinnerware

Mottahedeh Inc. (M)
225 Fifth Avenue
New York, NY 10010
18th-century
reproduction porcelain
dinnerware

Noritake (M)
41 Madison Avenue
New York, NY 10010
Casual dinnerware,
stoneware, stemware

Pewter Cupboard (M)
1776 Easton Road
Doylestown, PA 18901
Reproduction pewter
dinnerware, flatware,
lighting, mail-order
catalog

Pfaltzgraff (M)
PO Box 1069
York, PA 17405
Stoneware dinnerware
and cookware

Pierre Deux, Inc. (R)
353 Bleecker Street
New York, NY 10014
Dinnerware, traditional
country French cotton
fabrics

Quimper Faience, Inc.
(M,R)
141 Water Street
Stonington, CT 06378
Hand-painted French
dinnerware, pottery,
mail-order

**Rauschert Culinary
Editions** (M)
4 Wilton Avenue
PO Box 62
Norwalk, CT 06852
Decorative dinnerware,
oven stoneware

**Rosenthal China and
Crystal, USA** (M)
PO Box 1008
Des Plaines, IL 60018
Dinnerware

Rowantrees Pottery (M)
Blue Hill, ME 04614
Dinnerware, stoneware,
pottery, mail-order
catalog

**Royal Copenhagen
Porcelain/Georg
Jensen Silversmiths** (M)
683 Madison Avenue
New York, NY 10021
Scandinavian-design
porcelain dinnerware,
lead crystal, sterling
flatware, copper
cookware

Royal Doulton (M)
Cottontail Lane
Somerset, NJ 08873
Bone china, porcelain,
and earthenware
dinnerware, ovenware

**Royal Worcester
Spode Inc.** (M)
26 Kennedy Boulevard
East Brunswick, NJ
08816
Dinnerware, English
bone china,
earthenware and
procelain ovenware

Scafati & Co. (W)
225 Fifth Avenue
New York, NY 10010
Porcelain, ironstone,
and earthenware
dinnerware

Soovia Janis (M)
225 Fifth Avenue
New York, NY 10010
Glazed redware
dinnerware, cookware

Directory of Sources

Reed & Barton

Stauffer Pewterware (M)
707 West Brubaker
Valley Road
Lititz, PA 17543
Colonial reproduction
pewter dinnerware,
mail-order

Toscany Imports, Ltd. (W)
386 Park Avenue South
New York, NY 10016
Imported dinnerware,
glassware, stemware,
ceramic service pieces

Trend Pacific, Inc. (M)
507 Towne Avenue
Los Angeles, CA 90013
Dinnerware

**Villeroy & Boch,
USA** (M)
41 Madison Avenue
New York, NY 10010
Dinnerware, wall and
floor tiles

**Waechtersbach USA,
Inc.** (M)
8300 NE Underground
Drive
Kansas City, MO 64161
Earthenware
dinnerware in solid
colors and country
designs

Wedgwood, Inc. (M)
41 Madison Avenue
New York, NY 10010
Adams English
earthenware and
cookware

Wilton Armatele (M)
18th and Franklin
Streets
Columbia, PA 17512
Metal dinnerware and
accessories

**Wolfman-Gold &
Good Co.** (R)
484 Broome Street
New York, NY 10013
Dinnerware, flatware,
white linens

**Woodbury
Pewterers** (M)
860 Main Street South
Woodbury, CT 06798
Henry Ford Museum
pewter reproductions,
catalog

FABRICS

Laura Ashley, Inc. (R)
714 Madison Avenue
New York, NY 10021
Fabrics, curtains, linens,
dinnerware, tiles, wall
coverings, mail-order
catalog

Boussac of France (T)
979 Third Avenue,
Room 1618
New York, NY 10022
Fabrics

**Brunschwig & Fils,
Inc.** (T)
75 North White Plains
White Plains, NY 10603
Fabrics, wall coverings

Calico Corners (R)
681 East Main Street
Mount Kisco, NY
10549
Fabrics

Manuel Canovas (T)
979 Third Avenue
New York, NY 10022
Fabrics

Constance Carol (M)
PO Box 899
Building 21, Cordage
Park
Plymouth, MA 02360
Fabrics, tab curtains,
custom styles, stenciled
patterns

China Seas (T)
21 East 4th Street
New York, NY 10003
Fabrics, wall coverings

Cohama/Riverdale (M)
200 Madison Avenue
New York, NY 10016
Fabrics

Covington Fabrics (M)
267 Fifth Avenue
New York, NY 10016
Fabrics

Decorating Den (R)
5753 West 85th Street
Indianapolis, IN 46278
Fabrics, wall coverings

A. L. Diamont & Co. (M)
309 Commerce Drive
Exton, PA 19341
Fabrics, documentary
wallpapers, borders

**Eisenhart
Wallcoverings Co.** (M)
Box 464
Hanover, PA 17331
Traditional country
fabrics, coordinated wall
coverings

Fabric Barn (R)
2717 North Clark
Chicago, IL 60614
Calicos and decorating
fabrics

Fabrications (R)
1740 Massachusetts
Avenue
Cambridge, MA 02138
Fabrics

Gear, Inc. (M)
19 West 34th Street
New York, NY 10001
Fabric, wall coverings,
linens, dinnerware,
bakeware, furniture

Stark Carpet Corp.

S. M. Hexter, Co. (M)
979 Third Avenue,
Room 922
New York, NY 10022
Fabrics, wall coverings

Hinson & Company (T)
979 Third Avenue
New York, NY 10022
Fabrics, wall coverings

Homespun Weavers (M)
530 State Avenue
Emmaus, PA 18049
Fabrics, linens, catalog

**Jensen Lewis Co.,
Inc.** (M)
89 Seventh Avenue
New York, NY 10011
Fabrics, solid-color
canvases, catalog

**Ralph Lauren Home
Furnishings** (M)
1185 Avenue of the
    Americas
New York, NY 10019
Fabrics, linens,
dinnerware, flatware,
furniture

Jack Lenor Larsen (T)
41 East 11th Street
New York, NY 10003
Fabrics

Liberty of London (M)
108 West 39th Steet
New York, NY 10017
Fabrics, mail-order

Marimekko (R)
7 West 56th Street
New York, NY 10019
Fabrics, wall coverings,
kitchen textiles

Pierre Deux, Inc. (R)
353 Bleecker Street
New York, NY 10014
Traditional country
French cotton fabrics,
dinnerware

Quadrille (T)
979 Third Avenue
New York, NY 10022
Fabrics, wall coverings

Scalamandre (T)
37-24 24th Street
Long Island City, NY
11101
Fabrics

Schumacher & Co. (T)
939 Third Avenue
New York, NY 10022
Fabrics, wall coverings

Stroheim & Romann (T)
155 East 56th Street
New York, NY 10022
Fabrics

Waverly Fabrics (M)
58 West 40th Street
New York, NY 10018
Traditional fabrics and
wall coverings

FLATWARE

**The American Country
Store** (R)
969 Lexington Avenue
New York, NY 10021
Flatware, antique and
contemporary
dinnerware, decorative
accessories, table linens,
mail-order

Dansk Designs Ltd. (M)
Radio Circle Road
Mount Kisco, NY
10549
Stainless-steel flatware,
enamel dinnerware and
cookware

**Ginkgo International,
Ltd.** (W)
5107 Chase Street
Downers Grove, IL
60515
Imported stainless-steel
and melamine flatware,
dinnerware

Gorham (M)
333 Adelaide Avenue
Providence, RI 02907
Sterling flatware

Jori Hand Cast Pewter
(M,R)
Bucks County
Pewterers, Inc.
1776 Easton Road
Doylestown, PA 18901
Hand-cast pewter
flatware and dinnerware

Kirk Stieff Co. (M)
800 Wyman Park Drive
Baltimore, MD 21211
Sterling, silverplate,
pewter, stainless-steel
flatware

**Ralph Lauren Home
Furnishings** (M)
1185 Avenue of the
    Americas
New York, NY 10019
Flatware, dinnerware,
fabrics, linens, furniture

**Newton Millham Star
Forge** (R)
672 Drift Road
Westport, MA 02790
Cooking utensils,
custom reproduction
17th- and 18th-century
wrought-iron hardware,
hearth, lighting,
brochure

Oneida Silversmiths (M)
Oneida, NY 13421
Traditional sterling,
stainless-steel,
silverplate designs

Pennsylvania House

Oxford Hall Silversmiths (M)
225 Fifth Avenue
New York, NY 10010
Flatware

Pewter Cupboard (M)
1776 Easton Road
Doylestown, PA 18901
Reproduction pewter
flatware, dinnerware,
lighting, mail-order
catalog

Reed & Barton (M)
144 West Britannia
    Street
Taunton, MA 02780
Traditional silver,
pewter, stainless-steel
flatware styles

Royal Copenhagen Porcelain / Georg Jensen Silversmiths (M)
683 Madison Avenue
New York, NY 10021
Scandinavian-design
sterling flatware, copper
cookware, porcelain
dinnerware, lead crystal

Towle Silversmith Co. (M)
260 Merrimack Street
Newburyport, MA 01950
Traditional sterling
flatware

Wolfman-Gold & Good Co. (R)
484 Broome Street
New York, NY 10013
Flatware, dinnerware,
white linens

Marion Travis

Yamazaki Tableware, Inc. (M)
41 Madison Avenue
New York, NY 10010
Stainless-steel flatware

FLOORING

Adams and Swett (R)
380 Dorcester Avenue
Boston, MA 02127
Hand-braided wool rugs

Agency Tile Inc. (M)
979 Third Avenue
New York, NY 10022
Tile flooring

American Olean Tile (M)
PO Box 271
1000 Cannon Avenue
Lansdale, PA 19446
Tile flooring

Armstrong World Industries (M)
150 North Queen Street
PO Box 3001
Lancaster, PA 17604
Vinyl flooring

Laura Ashley, Inc. (R)
714 Madison Avenue
New York, NY 10021
Tiles, curtains, fabrics,
linens, dinnerware, wall
coverings, mail-order
catalog

Braid-Aid (R)
466 Washington Street
Pembroke, MA 02359
Rug-making supplies,
quilting, spinning,
catalog

Bruce Hardwood Flooring (M)
16803 Dallas Parkway
Dallas, TX 75248
70 hardwood
variations, mail-order

Buckingham-Virginia Slate Corp. (M)
PO Box 11002
Richmond, VA 23230
Slate flooring

Capel, Inc. (M)
PO Box 528
831 North Main Street
Troy, NJ 27371
Braided and hooked
rugs, dhurries, catalog

Coker Creek Crafts (M)
PO Box 95
Coker Creek, TN
37314
Rugs, white-oak
baskets, linens, catalog

Colonial Mills, Inc. (M)
560 Mineral Spring
    Avenue
Pawtucket, RI 02860
Braided rugs

Congoleum Corp. (M)
195 Belgrove Drive
Kearny, NJ 07032
Vinyl flooring

Country Floors (R)
300 East 61st Street
New York, NY 10021
Imported ceramic tile

Country Tiles (R)
194 Main Street
Westport, CT 06880
Imported ceramic tile

Elizabeth Eakins (R)
1053 Lexington
    Avenue
New York, NY 10021
Custom-made
handwoven, braided,
and hooked rugs; tiles,
trays, plates, trivets

Elon, Inc. (M)
150 East 58th Street
New York, NY 10155
Handmade imported tile

Pennsylvania House

Ms. Betty Emerson (R)
Greenwich Village Mall
109 Towne Road
Oak Ridge, TN 37830
One-of-a-kind rugs,
Swedish-lace place
mats, mail-order

Folk Art Floorcloths (R)
PO Box 431
Elm Grove, WI 53122
Original floorcloth
designs, old grocery-
store signs, catalog

**Andrea Guttman/
Bushman** (R)
2 Marble Terrace
Hastings-on-Hudson,
NY 10706
Custom rag rugs, mail-
order

Hall Place Tile Shop(R)
2231 Broadway
New York, NY 10024
Country-style hand-
painted ceramic tiles,
tile flooring,
countertops, wall
coverings

Hastings Tile (M)
30 Commercial Street
Freeport, NY 11520
Imported Italian tile

Heritage Rugs (M,R)
Peddler's Village
Lahaska, PA 18931
Custom-made
handwoven rag rugs,
brochure

Import Specialists (W)
82 Wall Street
New York, NY 10005
Hemp rugs, baskets,
linens, rag place mats

Kentile Floors, Inc. (M)
58 Second Avenue
Brooklyn, NY 11215
Resilient floor and
counter tile

**Mannington Mills,
Inc.** (M)
PO Box 30
Salem, NJ 08079
Vinyl flooring, resilient
sheet flooring

Mid-State Tile Co. (M)
PO Box 1777
Lexington, NC 27292
Ceramic tiles, tile
flooring

Mills River Industries (M)
713 Old Orchard Road
Hendersonville, NC
28739
Flat-braided rugs, split-
wood and root baskets,
linens, decorator
accessories

**Rastetter Woolen
Mill** (R)
Star Route, Box 42
Millersburg, OH 44654
Custom handwoven
rugs, mail-order

The Rug House (R)
PO Box 3042
Cincinnati, OH 45201
Braided and woven
wool rugs, mail-order

**Saxony Carpet Co.,
Inc.** (T)
979 Third Avenue
New York, NY 10022
Braided wool,
handwoven cotton rag,
and cotton-linen rugs,
dhurries, kilims, antique
Orientals

Stark Carpet Corp. (T)
979 Third Avenue
New York, NY 10022
Custom and stock
designs, area rugs,
carpets

Tarkett, Inc. (M)
PO Box 264
Parsippany, NJ 07054
Vinyl flooring

**Villeroy & Boch,
USA** (M)
41 Madison Avenue
New York, NY 10010
Floor and wall tiles,
dinnerware

FURNITURE

Added Oomph! (M)
PO Box 6135
High Point, NC 27262
Swamp-willow-branch
twig furniture

Angel House Designs
(M,R)
RFD 1, Box 1
Route 148
Brookfield, MA 01506
Reproduction colonial
tables, hutches,
chandeliers, chairs

Bittersweet (M)
PO Box 5
Riverton, VT 05668
Reproduction colonial
cupboards, harvest and
trestle tables, custom
work, brochure

**Douglas Campbell
Co.** (M)
PO Box 31
Buck's Harbor, ME
04618
Reproduction 17th- and
18th-century American
furniture, catalog

Chestnut Street Gallery (R)
319 Chestnut Street
PO Box 229
Berea, KY 40403
Custom and reproduction work, tables, hutches, stools, chairs

Colonial Williamsburg Foundation (M,R)
PO Box CH
Williamsburg,VA 23185
Documented furniture, hardware, decorator accessories, dinnerware from Williamsburg Collection, catalog, mail-order brochure

Cornucopia, Inc. (M)
PO Box 30-C
Wescott Road
Harvard, MA 01451
Handcrafted reproduction tables, hutches, chairs, accessories

The Country Bed Shop (R)
Box 222
Groton, MA 01450
Handcrafted 17th- and 18th-century-style cupboards, trestle and gateleg tables, chairs

The Ethan Allen Co. (M)
Ethan Allen Drive
Danbury, CT 06810
Reproduction Early American furniture

Simms Thayer

Gear, Inc. (M)
19 West 34th Street
New York, NY 10001
Furniture, dinnerware, cookware, fabric, wall coverings, linens

Habersham Plantation
PO Box 1209
Lot 5, Collier Road
Toccoa, GA 30577
17th- and 18th-century colonial reproduction tables, chairs, hutches

Hale of Vermont (M)
East Arlington,VT 05252
Maple, oak, cherry tables, chairs, hutches, catalog

Harden Furniture Co.(M)
Mill Pond Way
McConnellsville, NY 13401
Reproduction Early American tables, chairs, hutches

Hitchcock Furniture Co. (M)
New Hartford, CT 06057
Handcrafted and traditional furniture

Howard Kaplan's French Country Store (R)
35 East 10th Street
New York, NY 10003
French antique and reproduction furniture, dinnerware, accessories

The Lane Co. (M)
Box 151
East Franklin Avenue
Altavista, VA 24517
America Collection, reproduction dining tables and chairs, catalog

Ralph Lauren Home Furnishings (M)
1185 Avenue of the Americas
New York, NY 10019
Furniture, flatware, dinnerware, fabrics, linens

Thomas Moser, Cabinetmakers (M)
PO Box 128-L
New Gloucester, ME 04260
Handcrafted solid cherry furniture, catalog

Nichols & Stone (M)
232 Sherman Street
Gardner, MA 01440
Fine traditional furniture designs

J. F. Orr and Sons (M)
113 Village Green
Route 27
Sudbury, MA 01776
Furniture and accessories

Clyde Pearson (M)
1420 Progress Street
PO Box 2838
High Point, NC 27261
Museum of American Folk Art "Americana" collection

Pennsylvania House (M)
11th Street
Lewisburg, PA 17837
Dining chairs and tables, catalog

Shaker Workshops (M)
Box 1028
Concord, MA 01742
Reproduction Shaker furniture and accessories, catalog

The Silo (R)
Upland Road
New Milford, CT 06776
Furniture, baskets, one-of-a-kind crafts, catalog

Simms & Thayer Cabinetmakers (M)
PO Box 35
North Marshfield, MA 02059
Reproduction American country furniture

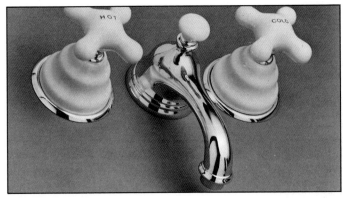

Renovator's Supply

Renovator's Supply

Telescope Folding Furniture (M)
Church Street
Granville, NY 12832
Wooden and aluminum casual furniture, director's chairs, cafe chairs, tables

Thomasville Furniture (M)
PO Box 339
Thomasville, NC 27360
Reproduction furniture

Marion Travis (R)
PO Box 292
Statesville, NC 28677
Hardwood chairs, woven rush-fiber seats

Triconfort (M)
119 West 57th Street
New York, NY 10019
Synthetic resin indoor/outdoor furniture

Yesterday's Yankee (M,R)
Lakeville, CT 06039
Reproduction 17th- to 19th-century Shaker tote stools, hutches, settle tables, mail-order

GLASSWARE

Anchor Hocking Corp. (M)
Fifth and Pierce Avenues
Lancaster, OH 43130
Stemware, cookware, dinnerware

Arabia, for Sigma the Tastesetter (M)
225 Fifth Avenue
New York, NY 10010
Glassware, woodenware, Finnish enamel cookware, and stoneware

Ball Corp. (M)
Consumer Products Division
345 South High Street
Muncie, IN 47305
Home canning jars and supplies

Cardinal China Co. (M)
Cardinal Building
High Street, Box D
Carteret, NJ 07008
Storage jars, gourmet accessories, white china dinnerware, earth-tone crocks, mail-order

Colony (M)
1115 Broadway
New York, NY 10010
Glassware, crystal

Crisa (M)
1201 Richardson Drive
Richardson, TX 75080
Glass dinnerware and stemware, old-fashioned jars and pitchers

Cristallerie Zwiesel (M)
3 Odell Plaza
Yonkers, NY 10701
Machine-cut stemware

Crown Corning Glassware (M)
3014 Tanager Avenue
Los Angeles, CA 90040
Glass- and stemware

Denby Tableware, Inc. (M)
130 Campus Plaza
Edison, NJ 08837
Glassware, stoneware dinnerware and cookware

J. G. Durand (M)
PO Box 200
Millville, NJ 08332
Lead-crystal stemware, clamp-top storage jars

Fenton Art Glass Co. (M)
700 Elizabeth Street
Williamstown, WV 26187
Handmade decorative glass, catalog

Fostoria Glass Co. (M)
1200 First Street
Moundsville, WV 26041
Glass stemware

iittala glassware (W)
41 Madison Avenue
New York, NY 10010
Finnish handmade glassware

Kerr Glass (M)
PO Box 97
Main Street
Sand Springs, OK 74063
Canning, freezing, storage jars

Libbey Glass (M)
One Seagate
Toledo, OH 43666
Glassware

Noritake (M)
41 Madison Avenue
New York, NY 10010
Casual stemware, dinnerware, stoneware

The Pilgrim Glass Corp. (M)
225 Fifth Avenue
New York, NY 10010
Glassware

Cassidy Brothers Forge

Authentic Designs

Royal Copenhagen Porcelain/Georg Jensen Silversmiths (M)
683 Madison Avenue
New York, NY 10021
Scandinavian-design lead crystal, sterling flatware, copper cookware, porcelain dinnerware

St. Gobain Glassware (M)
41 Madison Avenue
New York, NY 10010
French tempered glassware and ovenware

Toscany Imports, Ltd. (W)
386 Park Avenue South
New York, NY 10016
Imported glassware, dinnerware, stemware, ceramic service pieces

Viking Glass Co. (M)
802 Parkway
PO Box 29
New Martinsville, WV 26155
Handcrafted crystal, catalog

VMC French Glassware (W)
PO Box 639
Stamford, CT 06904
French storage jars, tabletop accessories

West Virginia Glass Co. (M)
Drawer 510
Weston, WV 26452
Handcrafted crystal glassware

Wheaton Fine Glass (M)
1501 North 10th Street
Millville, NJ 08332
Glassware, storage jars, stemware

HARDWARE

Ajax Hardware (M)
825 South Ajax Avenue
City of Industry, CA 91749
General hardware accessories

Baldwin Hardware Corporation (M)
Box 82
841 Wyomissing Boulevard
Reading, PA 19603
Solid brass traditional hardware and lighting

Ball and Ball (M)
463 West Lincoln Highway
Exton, PA 19341
Reproduction (1700-1900) hardware, custom work available, catalogs

Bear Creek Forge (M)
Route 2, Box 135
Spring Green, WI 53588
Hand-forged ceiling pot racks, paper-towel racks, stoves, andirons

Cassidy Brothers Forge (M)
Route 1
Rowley, MA 01969
Custom metalwork, gates, reproduction hardware, lighting

Colonial Williamsburg Foundation (M)
PO Box CH
Williamsburg, VA 23185
Hardware, dinnerware from Williamsburg Collection, decorator accessories, documented furniture, catalog, mail-order brochure

The Decorator Emporium and Hardware, Inc. (R)
353 Main Street
Danbury, CT 06810
Reproduction hardware, mail-order

Forms + Surfaces (M)
Box 5215
Santa Barbara, CA 93108
Kitchen hardware

Horton Brasses (M)
Nooks Hill Road
PO Box 120CL
Cromwell, CT 06146
Reproduction 17th- to 20th-century pulls, catalog

Steve Kayne Hand Forged Hardware (R)
17 Harmon Place
Smithtown, NY 11787
Kitchen hardware

Kirsch Products (M)
PO Box 0370
309 North Prospect Avenue
Sturgis, MI 49091
Drapery hardware, blinds, shades

Charles Lapen (R)
Route 9, PO Box 529
West Brookfield, MA 01585
Custom wrought-iron hardware and chandeliers, hand-forged cutlery, mail-order

The Wicker Warehouse

Newton Millham Star Forge (R)
672 Drift Road
Westport, MA 02790
Custom reproduction
17th- and 18th-century
wrought-iron hardware,
hearth, cooking utensils,
lighting, brochure

Omnia Industries Inc. (M)
PO Box 263
49 Park Street
Montclair, NJ 07042
Hardware and kitchen
accessories

The Renovator's Supply, Inc. (R)
6017 Renovator's
   Old Mill
Millers Falls, MA 01349
Iron hardware, repro-
duction brass, catalog

Southbound Millworks (M)
PO Box 349
Sandwich, MA 02563
Wood and wrought-iron
hardware, mail-order

Virginia Metalcrafters, Inc. (M)
PO Box 1068
Waynesboro, VA
22980
Reproduction brass,
cast-iron accessories,
tin lighting fixtures

Wallin Forge (R)
Route 1, Box 65
Sparta, KY 41086
Custom work, forged
iron pot racks

HERBS

Applewood Seed Co. (R)
PO Box 10761
Edgemont Station
Golden, CO 80401
Herb seeds

Burpee's Seeds (R)
Box B02001
Clinton, IA 52732
Herb seeds and plants

Ceres Garden (R)
PO Box 6247
Providence, RI 02940
Herb seeds

Faith Mountain Country Fare (R)
Main Street
PO Box 199
Sperryville, VA 22740
Herbs and accessories,
catalog

Gilbertis (W)
Sylvan Lane
Westport, CT 06880
Herb plants, wreaths,
catalog

The Herb Patch (R)
Apple Pie Farm
Union Hill Road, RD 1
Malvern, PA 19355
Fresh herbs, basket
arrangements, wreaths,
mail-order

Meadowbrook Herb Garden (R)
Wyoming, RI 02898
Herb seeds and plants

George W. Park Seed Co. (R)
PO Box 31
Greenwood, SC 29646
Herb seeds

Stillridge Herb Farm (R)
10370 Route 99
Woodstock, MD 21163
Herbs, wreaths, mail-
order catalog

Stokes Seeds, Inc. (R)
737 Main Street
Buffalo, NY 14240
Herb seeds

KITCHEN FIXTURES

American Standard, Inc. (M)
PO Box 2003
New Brunswick, NJ
08903
Enambled cast-iron and
stainless-steel sinks,
faucets

Casablanca Fan Co. (M)
450 North Baldwin Park
   Boulevard
City of Industry, CA
91746
Kitchen fixtures, ceiling
fans, catalog

Chicago Faucet (M)
2100 South Nuclear
   Drive
Des Plaines, IL 60018
Faucets

Delta Faucet Co. (M)
55 East 111th Street
PO Box 40980
Indianapolis, IN 46280
Faucets

Eljer Manufacturing Co. (M)
3 Gateway Center
Pittsburgh, PA 15222
Enameled sinks, faucets

Elkay Manufacturing Co. (M)
2222 Camden Court
Oak Brook, IL 60521
Kitchen fixtures

Heritage Lanterns (M)
70A Main Street
Yarmouth, ME 04096
Handcrafted reproduction copper, brass, and pewter lighting fixtures, mail-order catalog

Kohler Co. (M)
Kohler, WI 53044
Fixtures, enameled sinks, faucets

The Tile Shop (M)
1005 Harrison Street
Berkeley, CA 94710
Kitchen fixtures, ceramic tiles, hand-thrown stoneware and porcelain sinks

KITCHEN TEXTILES

The American Country Store (R)
969 Lexington Avenue
New York, NY 10021
Table linens, flatware, antique and contemporary dinnerware, decorative accessories, mail-order

Kemp & Beatley, Inc.

Beaumont Pottery

Laura Ashley, Inc. (R)
714 Madison Avenue
New York, NY 10021
Linens, curtains, fabrics, tiles, dinnerware, wall coverings, mail-order catalog

Barth & Dreyfuss (M)
2260 East 15th Street
Los Angeles, CA 90021
Linens

Cannon Mills (M)
1271 Avenue of the
    Americas
New York, NY 10020
Kitchen textiles in country motifs

Coker Creek Crafts (M)
PO Box 95
Coker Creek, TN 37314
Linens, rugs, white-oak baskets, catalog

Ms. Betty Emerson (R)
Greenwich Village Mall
109 Towne Road
Oak Ridge, TN 37380
Swedish-lace place mats, one-of-a-kind rugs, mail-order

Gear, Inc. (M)
19 West 34th Street
New York, NY 10001
Linens, fabric, wall coverings, furniture, dinnerware, cookware

Goodwin Weavers/ Blowing Rock Crafts, Inc. (M,R)
PO Box 314
Blowing Rock, NC 28605
Cotton honeycomb place mats and napkins, catalog

Homespun Weavers (M)
530 State Avenue
Emmaus, PA 18049
Linens and fabrics, catalog

Ilonka (R)
PO Box 5964
Carmel, CA 93921
American country place mats, French tablecloths and linens

Import Specialists (W)
82 Wall Street
New York, NY 10005
Linens, rag place mats, hemp rugs, baskets

Le Jacquard Français, Inc. (M)
200 Lovers Lane
Culpepper, VA 22701
French damask table linens

Kangaroo Line (M)
c/o Susan O'Kane Inc.
27 Flamingo Plaza
Hialeah, FL 33010
Kitchen linens, place mats, napkins

Katja Design Services, Inc. (M)
466 Washington Street
New York, NY 10013
Kitchen and table linens, vinyl and woven textiles

Kemp & Beatley (M)
1040 Avenue of the
    Americas
New York, NY 10018
Tablecloths, napkins, place mats

Hartstone, Inc.

Ralph Lauren Home Furnishings (M)
1185 Avenue of the Americas
New York, NY 10019
Linens, fabrics, furniture, flatware, dinnerware

Leacock & Co., Inc. (M)
1040 Avenue of the Americas
New York, NY 10018
Kitchen and tabletop linens

Marimekko (R)
7 West 56th Street
New York, NY 10019
Kitchen textiles, fabrics, wall coverings

Paper White Ltd. (M)
769 Center Boulevard
Faifax, CA 94930
Hand-embroidered aprons, napkins, tablecloths

Puckihuddle Products, Ltd. (R)
Main Street
Phoenicia, NY 12464
Table linens, patchwork place mats, napkins

John Ritzenthaler Co. (M)
40 Portland Road
West Conshohocken, PA 19428
Kitchen textiles, dish towels, aprons, potholders

Flossie Samuels (W)
123 East 37th Street
New York, NY 10016
Oversized lace trim, ikat print, French provincial napkins, runners, tablecloths, custom orders

Sel-Bar Weaving, Inc. (M)
PO Box 759
Newport, VT 05855
Handwoven cotton place mats
Mail-order address:
Vermont Textiles Co.
PO Box 192
Derby, VT 05829

Ulster Weaving Corp. Ltd. (M)
148 Madison Avenue
New York, NY 10016
Linen towels in windowpane checks and stripes

Wolfman-Gold & Good Co. (R)
484 Broome Street
New York, NY 10013
White linens, flatware, dinnerware

LIGHTING

Abolite Lighting Co., Inc. (M)
305 North Center
West Lafayette, OH 43845
incandescent lighting

Authentic Designs (M)
The Mill Road
West Rupert, VT 05776
Reproduction Early American lighting, catalog

Baldwin Hardware Corporation (M)
Box 82
841 Wyomissing Boulevard
Reading, PA 19603
Solid brass traditional lighting and hardware

Cassidy Brothers Forge (M)
Route 1
Rowley, MA 01969
Reproduction lighting, hardware, custom metalwork, gates

The Essex Forge (R)
5K Old Dennison Road
Essex, CT 06426
Hand-wrought tin and iron chandeliers, sconces, lamps, lanterns, catalog

Halo Lighting Division (M)
McGraw Edison Co.
40 Busse Road
Elk Grove Village, IL 60007
Track lighting

Heritage Lanterns (M)
70A Main Street
Yarmouth, ME 04096
Handcrafted reproduction copper, brass, and pewter lighting fixtures, mail-order catalog

Rowe Pottery Works

Beaumont Pottery

Hubbardton Forge and Wood Corp. (M)
RD 1
Fair Haven, VT 05743
Colonial reproduction lighting, custom work available, mail-order catalog

Charles Lapen (R)
Route 9, PO Box 529
West Brookfield, MA 01585
Custom wrought-iron chandeliers and lighting, hand-forged cutlery, mail-order

Newton Millham Star Forge (R)
672 Drift Road
Westport, MA 02790
Lighting, cooking utensils, custom reproduction 17th- and 18th-century wrought-iron hardware, hearth, brochure

North Country Shades (M,R)
Fletcher Road, RFD 1
Box 210
Newport, RI 03773
Pierced lampshades, traditional and country designs, catalog

Period Lighting Fixtures (M)
1 Main Street
Chester, CT 06412
Handmade reproduction lighting fixtures, catalog

Pewter Cupboard (M)
1776 Easton Road
Doylestown, PA 18901
Reproduction pewter lighting, dinnerware, flatware, mail-order catalog

Robelier (M)
1500 South 50th Street
Philadelphia, PA 19143
Lighting products, mail-order catalog

The Tin Bin (M)
20 Valley Road
Neffsville, PA 17601
18th- and 19th-century handcrafted tin, copper, and brass lighting, catalog

Tin Peddlar (M)
5325 Horseshoe Bend Road
Troy, OH 45373
Handcrafted, reproduction lighting, sconces, lanterns, chandeliers, mail-order catalog

Unique Lighting (M)
PO Box 1085
480 Jefferson Avenue
Morrisville, PA 19067
Tiffany-style shades, brochure

Virginia Metalcrafters, Inc. (M)
PO Box 1068
Waynesboro, VA 22980
Tin lighting fixtures, reproduction brass, cast-iron accessories

Lt. Moses Willard, Inc. (M)
7805 Railroad Avenue
Cincinnati, OH 45243
Reproduction colonial and folk-art lighting fixtures, chandeliers, sconces

PAINTS

Benjamin Moore Paints (M)
51 Chestnut Ridge Road
Montvale, NJ 07645
Paints and stains, selection of historic colors

Cohasset Colonials (M)
245X Ship Street
Cohasset, MA 02025
Reproduction 18th- and 19th-century milk-based paints

Kosta Boda

Pfaltzgraff

Finnaren and Haley, Inc. (M,R)
2320 Haverford Road
Ardmore, PA 19003
Paint in colors of historic Philadelphia

The Old Fashioned Milk Paint Co. (M)
Box 222
Groton, MA 01450
Old-fashioned milk-based paints, wide pine flooring and cabinet boards

The Olympic Homecare Products Co. (M)
2233 112th Avenue N.E.
Bellevue, WA 98004
Traditional paints and stains

Sherwin Williams (R)
(Consult telephone directory for local distributor)
Paints and wall coverings

POTTERY

Artique (M)
30-C Maple Avenue
Waldwick, NJ 07463
19th-century reproduction gray pottery with cobalt decorations

Beaumont Heritage Pottery (M)
293 Beach Ridge Road
York, ME 03909
Reproduction pottery, cobalt-decorated salt-glazed stoneware

Boston Warehouse (M)
39 Rumford Avenue
Waltham, MA 02154
Pottery, stoneware, bowls, bakeware

Breininger Pottery (M)
476 South Church Street
Robesonia, PA 19551
Earthenware dinnerware, catalog

Brookville Potter (R)
Box 848
Brookville Hollow Road
Stockton, NJ 08559
Pottery, stoneware, cookware, dinnerware, sponge ware

Anne Burnham and Gary Quirk Potters (M)
HCR 84, Box 5
Picketville Road
Parishville, NY 13672
Pottery, hand-thrown stoneware

The Country Store (R)
28 James Street
Geneva, IL 60134
Pottery, enamelware, stenciled stoneware, accessories, mail-order

Crate & Barrel (R)
190 Northfield Road
Northfield, IL 60093
Pottery, cookware, catalog

The Elements Pottery (R)
629 North 3rd Street
Denville, KY 40422
Pottery, blue and beige stoneware, mail-order

Pepper Fewel (M)
5803 Galloway Drive
Yakima, WA 98908
Pottery, whimsical hand-thrown and sculptured bakeware, mail-order

The Foltz Pottery (M)
RD 1, Box 131
Reinholds, PA 17569
Pottery, cookware, catalog

Livingston Pottery (R)
Box 74
Livingston, NY 12541
Pottery, earthenware and porcelain bake-ware, mail-order catalog

New Geneva Stoneware Co. (M)
Box 649
Masontown, PA 15461
Hand-thrown and decorated pottery and stoneware, mail-order catalog

Kosta Boda

The Potting Shed (R)
43 Bradford Street
PO Box 1287
Concord, MA 01742
Dedham reproduction
pottery, crackle glaze,
catalog

Quimper Faience, Inc.
(M,R)
141 Water Street
Stonington, CT 06378
Hand-painted French
pottery, dinnerware,
mail-order

**The Robinson-
Ramsbottom Pottery
Co.** (M)
Roseville, OH 43777
Pottery, stoneware,
mail-order catalog

Rowantrees Pottery (M)
Blue Hill, ME 04614
Pottery, stoneware,
dinnerware, mail-order
catalog

Rowe Pottery Works
(M,R)
404 England Street
Cambridge, WI 53523
Hand-thrown pottery,
salt-glazed stoneware,
catalog

Ron Taylor Pottery (R)
10800 East 24 Highway
Sugar Creek, MO
64054
Pottery, stoneware,
kitchenware, mail-order
catalog

STONEWARE

**Arabia, for Sigma the
Tastesetter** (M)
225 Fifth Avenue
New York, NY 10010
Stoneware, Finnish
enamel cookware,
glassware, woodenware

**Beaumont Heritage
Pottery** (M)
293 Beach Ridge Road
York, ME 03909
Cobalt-decorated salt-
glazed stoneware,
reproduction pottery

**Bennington Potters
North** (M)
PO Box 199
324 County Street
Bennington, VT 05201
Stoneware, cookware,
accessories, catalog

**Bing & Grondahl
Copenhagen
Porcelain, Inc.** (M)
111 North Lawn
   Avenue
Elmsford, NY 10523
Danish stoneware and
porcelain dinnerware

Boston Warehouse (M)
39 Rumford Avenue
Waltham, MA 02154
Stoneware, pottery,
cookware, bowls

Brookville Pottery (R)
Box 848
Brookville Hollow Road
Stockton, NJ 08559
Stoneware cookware
and dinnerware,
sponge ware

**Anne Burnham and
Gary Quirk Potters** (M)
HCR 84, Box 5
Picketville Road
Parishville, NY 13672
Hand-thrown
stoneware, pottery

The Country Store (R)
28 James Street
Geneva, IL 60134
Stenciled stoneware,
pottery, enamelware,
accessories, mail-order

Delaware Pottery (M)
PO Box 105
Hope, NJ 07844
Handmade blue-and-
white traditional
stoneware, cookware

**The Elements
Pottery** (R)
629 North 3rd Street
Denville, KY 40422
Blue and beige
stoneware, pottery,
mail-order

Hartstone, Inc. (M)
PO Box 2626
Zanesville, OH 43701
Stoneware, clay
bakeware, dinnerware
**Iron Mountain
Stoneware** (M)
Laurel Bloomery, TN
37680
Stoneware oven- and
dinnerware, hand-
painted tiles
**New Geneva
Stoneware Co.** (M)
Box 649
Masontown, PA 15461
Hand-thrown and
decorated stoneware
and pottery, mail-order
catalog
Noritake (M)
41 Madison Avenue
New York, NY 10010
Casual stoneware,
dinnerware, stemware
Pfaltzgraff (M)
PO Box 1069
York, PA 17405
Stoneware dinnerware
and cookware
**Rauschert Culinary
Editions** (M)
4 Wilton Avenue
PO Box 62
Norwalk, CT 06852
Oven stoneware,
decorative dinnerware

Pfaltzgraff

**The Robinson-
Ramsbottom Pottery
Co.** (M)
Roseville, OH 43777
Stoneware, pottery,
mail-order catalog
Rowantrees Pottery (M)
Blue Hill, ME 04614
Stoneware, pottery,
dinnerware, mail-order
catalog
Rowe Pottery Works
(M,R)
404 England Street
Cambridge, WI 53523
Salt-glazed stoneware,
hand-thrown pottery,
catalog
Ron Taylor Pottery (R)
10800 East 24 Highway
Sugar Creek, MO
64054
Stoneware, pottery,
kitchenware, mail-order
catalog

WALL COVERINGS
Adele Bishop (R)
Box 3349
Kinston, NC 28501
Stencil kits for walls and
floor, catalog
Laura Ashley, Inc. (R)
714 Madison Avenue
New York, NY 10021
English country wall
coverings, linens, tiles,
curtains, fabrics,
dinnerware, mail-order
catalog
**Brunschwig & Fils,
Inc.** (T)
75 Virginia Road
White Plains, NY
Wall coverings, fabrics
China Seas (T)
21 East 4th Street
New York, NY 10003
Wall coverings, fabrics
**Columbus Coated
Fabrics** (M)
1280 North Grant
Avenue
Columbus, OH 43216
Walltex papers

Decorating Den (R)
5753 West 85th Street
Indianapolis, IN 46278
Wall coverings, fabrics
**A. L. Diamont &
Co.** (M)
309 Commerce Drive
Exton, PA 19341
Documentary borders,
wallpapers, fabrics
**Eisenhart
Wallcoverings Co.** (M)
Box 464
Hanover, PA 17331
Traditional country wall
coverings, coordinated
fabrics
Essex Wallcovering (M)
401 Hackensack
    Avenue
Hackensack, NJ 07601
Country French and
Early American wall
coverings
**Fashion
Wallcoverings** (M)
401 Hackensack
    Avenue
Hackensack, NJ 07601
Country French and
Early American wall
coverings
Gear, Inc. (M)
19 West 34th Street
New York, NY 10001
Wall coverings, linens,
furniture, dinnerware,
cookware, fabric

Hall Place Tile Shop (R)
2231 Broadway
New York, NY 10024
Wall coverings, countertops, country-style hand-painted ceramic tiles, tile flooring

S. M. Hexter Wallpaper (M)
2800 Superior Avenue
Cleveland, OH 44114
Early American-style wall coverings

Hinson and Co. (T)
979 Third Avenue
New York, NY 10022
Coordinated wall coverings and fabric

Imperial Wallcoverings (M)
23645 Mercantile Road
Cleveland, OH 44122
Early American and country-style wall coverings, stenciled papers

Lennon Wallpaper Co. (M)
PO Box 8
Joliet, IL 60436
Prepasted, vinyl-coated, dry-strippable wall coverings

Marimekko (R)
7 West 56th Street
New York, NY 10019
Wall coverings, kitchen textiles, fabrics

Jacques Jugeat, Inc.

Motif Designs (M)
15 Beechwood Avenue
New Rochelle, NY 10801
Wall coverings, mailorder

National Gypsum Co. (M)
Decorative Products
  Division
Corporate Place 128
Building 3
Suite 25
Wakefield, MA 01880
Straham, Benchmark, Style-Tex, Country Cupboard wallpapers

Prelude Designs (M)
One Hayes Street
Elmsford, NY 10523
Wall coverings, fabrics

Quadrille (T)
979 Third Avenue
New York, NY 10022
Wall coverings, fabrics

Sunworthy Wallcoverings (M)
195 Walker Drive
Brampton, Ontario, Canada L6T 329
Four collections of country kitchen wall coverings

Villeroy & Boch, USA (M)
41 Madison Avenue
New York, NY 10010
Wall and floor tiles, dinnerware

Waverly Fabrics (M)
58 West 40th Street
Traditional wall coverings and fabrics

York Wallcoverings, Inc. (M)
750 Linden Avenue
York, PA 17404
Prepasted, strippable, scrubbable, vinyl-coated wall coverings

WINDOWS

Andersen Windows (M)
Bayport, MN 55003
Windows

Combination Door Co. (M)
PO Box 1076
Fond du Lac, WI 54935
Windows

The House Carpenters (M)
Box 217
Shutesbury, MA 01072
Traditional red-oak and white-pine timber windows, frames, 18th-century flooring, molding, paneling, doors and doorways

Joanna Western Mills Co. (M)
2141 South Jefferson
Chicago, IL 60616
Wooden blinds, shades, shutters

Lord & Burnham (M)
Box 255
Irvington, NY 10533
Window greenhouses, greenhouses, solariums

Maurer and Sheperd, Joyners (M)
122 Naubuc Avenue
Glastonbury, CT 06033
18th-century reproduction muntin-style windows and millwork

Rolscreen Co. (M)
100 Main Street
Pella, IA 50219
Pella wood and aluminum windows, doors, skylights

Velux-America, Inc. (M)
PO Box 3208
Greenwood, SC 29648
Wood windows, skylights

WOOD-BURNING AND COAL STOVES

Ashley Heater Co. (M)
PO Box 128
Florence, AL 35630
Wood stoves

Atlanta Stove-works/Birmingham Stove & Range Co. (M)
PO Box 5254
Atlanta, GA 30307
Freestanding and cast-iron wood-burning and coal-burning stoves

Bow and Arrow Stove Co. (R)
11 Hurley Street
Cambridge, MA 02141
Coal and wood-burning stoves, mail-order

Capitol Export Corp. (M)
"Waterford Stanley Stove"
8825 Page Boulevard
St. Louis, MO 63114
Wood stoves

Ceramic Radiant Heat (M)
Department 2048
Pleasant Drive
Lochmere, NH 03252
Ceramic tiled wood-burning stoves, brochure

Vermont Castings, Inc.

Comforter Stove Works (M)
Box 188
Lochmere, NH 03252
Cast-iron parlor stove with cooktop

Consolidated Dutchwest (M)
Industrial Park Road
PO Box 1019
Plymouth, MA 02360
Wood-burning stoves

Crane Stoves Inc. (M)
PO Box 440
Braintree, MA 02184
Soapstone and coal-burning stoves, catalog

The Earth Stove, Inc. (M)
Tualatin, OR 97062
Wood stoves

Elmira Stove Works (M)
22 Church Street West
Elmira, Ontario,
Canada N3B 1M3
Wood stoves, mailorder

Godin Stoves (M)
Stone Ledge Co.
170 Washington Street
Marblehead, MA 01945
Wood stoves

Hearthstone II, Inc. (M)
RFD 1
Hearthstone Way
Morrisville, VT 05661
Wood stoves

Heatilator (M)
1915 West Saunders Road
Mount Pleasant, IA 52641
Wood stoves

Lopi International Ltd. (M)
10850 South 117th Place NE
Kirkland, WA 98033
Wood stoves

Majestic Stoves/Division of American Standard (M)
1000 East Market Street
Huntington, IN 46750
Masonry fireplace products

Rohn Stoves (M)
6718 West Plank Road
PO Box 2000
Peoria, IL 61656
Wood stoves

Russo Wood Stove Manufacturing Corp. (M)
87 Warren Street
Randolph, MA 02368
Catalytic stoves and fireplace inserts

Shenandoah Manufacturing Co., Inc. (M)
PO Box 839
Harrisonburg, VA 22801
Wood stoves

Sierra Manufacturing, Inc. (M)
PO Box 1089
Harrisonburg, VA 22801
Freestanding and hearth wood-burning stoves

Svendborg Co. (M)
Box 5
Hanover, NH 03755
Wood stoves
**U.S. Stove
Company** (M)
South Pittsfield, TN
37380
Wood stoves
**Vasto Woodburning
Products** (M)
PO Box 91
Hilton, NY 14468
Wood stoves
**Vermont Castings,
Inc.** (M)
Prince Street
Randolph, VT 05060
Cast-iron stoves,
brochure
**Washington Stove
Works** (M)
3402 Smith
PO Box 687
Everett, WA 98201
Early American wood-
or coal-burning range
Webster Stove (M)
3112 La Salle
St. Louis, MO 63104
Decorative wood-
burning parlor stoves
**Woodstock Soapstone
Co., Inc.** (M)
Route 4, Box 223
Woodstock, VT 05091
Cast-iron and soapstone
wood-burning stoves

Adele Bishop Inc. (Photo: Christian Carone)

WOODENWARE

J. K. Adams Co. (M)
PO Box 248
Dorset, VT 05251
Wooden chopping
blocks and tables
**Harriett Amanda
Chapman** (R)
331 East Main Street
Middletown, CT 06457
Woodenware,
mail-order
**Arabia, for Sigma the
Tastesetter** (M)
225 Fifth Avenue
New York, NY 10010
Woodenware, Finnish
enamel cookware,
stoneware, glassware
**Country Wood
Products, Inc.** (M)
510 Second Avenue
Wayland, NY 14572
Bowls and chopping
boards, mail-order
catalog

**Deerfield
Woodworking** (M)
PO Box 275
Deerfield, MA 01342
Curtain rods, paper-
towel racks, trivets,
mail-order
Foley-Martens Co. (M)
3300 Northeast Fifth
   Street
Minneapolis, MN 55418
Woodenware, kitchen
accessories
**HOAN Products
Ltd.** (M)
1595 MacArthur Blvd.
Mahwah, NJ 07430
Woodenware and
kitchen utensils
**Old Sturbridge
Village** (R)
Route 20 West
Sturbridge, MA 01566
Imported woodenware,
tinware molds
Tree Spirit (M)
Box 1920
Brattleboro, VT 05301
Wooden bowls, uten-
sils, soapstone griddles